7240 Arbol Dr.
Rockford Mi 49341

874-9349

THE MISUNDERSTOOD CHILD

THE MISUNDER-STOOD CHILD

*A Guide for Parents of Learning Disabled Children
by Larry B. Silver, M.D.*

McGRAW-HILL BOOK COMPANY

*New York   St. Louis   San Francisco
Hamburg   Mexico   Toronto*

2 3 4 5 6 7 8 9 DOC DOC 8 7 6 5

ISBN 0-07-057301-8

LIBRARY OF CONGRESS CATALOGING IN PUBLICATION DATA

Silver, Larry B.
The misunderstood child.
Includes index.
1. Learning disabilities.   I. Title.
RJ506.L4S55   1984   618.92′8   83-26839
ISBN 0-07-057301-8

This book is dedicated to

THE CENTER SCHOOL, Warren, New Jersey

To its director, Helen Goldberg, and the dedicated professional
staff for teaching me about these children;
To the children, who shared with me their feelings, thoughts,
fears, and hopes;
And, to the former social worker, R. Joan Guilmartin, who
taught me the importance of the family.

Thank you.

Preface

When a child or adolescent has learning disabilities, it interferes not only with academic work, but with all aspects of life—at home, in the community, in clubs, and in activities.

You, as parents, play a critical role in helping your child or adolescent deal with these disabilities. You must be an *informed consumer*, knowing all that is known about these problems. You must be an *assertive advocate*, constantly trying to find the programs your child needs in school, at home, and out of school. This book will help you to become both.

I have also tried to help you help the other members of your family. As you know all too well, when your son or daughter with learning disabilities feels pain, everyone feels it. I discuss your feelings, problems, and needs, as well as the impact that the learning disabled child or adolescent has on his or her brothers and sisters.

A child or adolescent with learning disabilities needs special understanding, support, and help from the family. This book should help you to be that special parent, and your family to be that special family.

Rockville, Maryland   Larry B. Silver, M.D.

The joy of learning is often a nightmare for more than 10 million normal, bright, intelligent children—just because no one has recognized their learning difference. Understand their frustration—and begin to understand the problem.

Let no child be demeaned, nor have his wonder diminished, because of our ignorance or inactivity. Let no child be deprived of discovery because we lack the resources to discover his or her problem. Let no child—ever—doubt self or mind because we are unsure of our commitment.

The Foundation for Children
with Learning Disabilities

Contents

Part One

An Introduction to the Learning Disabilities

1

Your Task as a Parent

Victor was a disaster in elementary school. He never sat still or paid attention in class, yet his teachers passed him along from grade to grade. By the fourth grade, when he was ten, he still read at a first-grade level, and his math skills were no better. The school evaluated him and concluded that he had learning disabilities. The report also described Victor as "hyperactive" and "distractible." Despite this evaluation, Victor went into a regular fifth-grade program. There his classroom and academic performance became even worse, and he also grew much more unpleasant and provocative at home.

By the time he finished the sixth grade, Victor could only be described as impossible. At school he did everything he knew of to get kicked out of class: he hid under desks, threw things, and crawled around the floor barking like a dog. All of his disruptive tactics succeeded. The kids thought he was funny, and he spent more time banished from the classroom than he spent in it.

The more trouble he got into at school, the more his parents tried to punish him at home. Soon the family was in chaos. When Victor rebelled against the limits his parents set as punishment, the parents fought with each other about how firm to be in enforcing them. His brother, already humiliated by Victor's behavior, spent more and more time at a friend's house to avoid the fighting at home. When the parents went to the school to try to get to the bottom of all this, the principal told them that Victor's emotional disturbance probably stemmed from their own marital distress. She told them that the school could not be responsible for family problems and suggested that they go for psychiatric help. No one mentioned the fourth-grade evaluation.

By the time the parents did seek a full private evaluation, Victor was almost thirteen years old. During the interviews, Victor's behavior shifted between quiet depression and open hostility. When quiet, he spoke of "being stupid." "I can't read good . . . I can't do anything good. . . . Maybe I'm just dumb." He saw himself as "bad." He was "ruining the family." "Maybe they should just send me away to school so I won't cause so much trouble." When he became hostile, Victor joked around, tried to break things in the office, and threatened to leave the room.

A new educational evaluation, updating the one done in the fourth grade, revealed multiple learning and language disabilities. Victor was three years behind in most skill areas. Psychological testing revealed a superior intellectual potential—a verbal IQ of 132—but a below-average performance IQ of 98. Everyone who took part in the evaluation saw him as Hyperactive and Distractible. The recommendations unanimously included: (1) placement in a fulltime special education program; (2) individual and family therapy; and (3) a trial on medication—that is, on psychostimulants.

I met with Victor to review the findings. He paraded in, joking about what "some dumb teacher" had done. I put my arm around his shoulder and said, "I want to let you know what *all* of the tests show. You know, now that I understand your problems, I really admire you. I'd probably have thrown in the towel years before you did." Victor sat down looking sad. But he followed me with interest as I reviewed his strong and weak areas, interrupting to make comments such as "You mean like when I read a page but forget what I read or I start to talk to someone and half way through I forget where I started?" I then went over the IQ test, subtest by subtest, showing him how particular learning problems interfered with his ability to answer the questions successfully. I emphasized how bright he was, and in what respects.

Later in our interview, I told Victor that I thought he had become the class clown to cover up for his being a "retard." I told him that

I didn't blame him, but that he could expect better of himself. Then I explained the proposed plan for special help. He understood what I described, but he refused to go along with it because he didn't want to go to a different school than his friends. I also explained why I wanted him to try medication and described what it could do. He didn't like that idea either, but he agreed to try it "for a few days." As he left my office, I reassured him that I understood the pain and frustration he had gone through and that I really wanted to help him. He smiled and held out his hand. We shook hands, and Victor left.

I reviewed the full evaluation and the series of recommendations once again in my meeting with Victor's parents. They seemed relieved to gain a better understanding of their son's difficulties than they had had, but they were angry with the school and with themselves for not doing something sooner. They agreed with all of the recommendations.

The next meeting was a family session with Victor, his brother, his parents, and his maternal grandmother who lived with the family. We reviewed the whole evaluation again. But during this session, Victor behaved very provocatively, and eventually forced everyone to get angry with him. I pointed out to him what he was doing and the effect it was having, but he continued with his irritating, disruptive behavior.

After a series of meetings with the personnel at Victor's school during which all of the data were again presented and discussed, it was agreed that Victor would go into a self-contained special educational program, a program in which he was to remain for the next three years although we did not know that then.

Victor's problems were serious, but not as severe as those of many such children, and certainly not hopeless. If you have a learning disabled child in your family, no doubt you recognize some of the elements in Victor's story. You can probably tell a more vivid, dramatic, and agonizing story yourself. If the learning disabled child is *your* child, no doubt you also know just how Victor's parents felt—their denial, frustration, anxiety, depression, guilt, and despair. And you probably recognize best of all their anger—anger at Victor, at the school, at each other; anger at the system, anger at the circumstance, and, perhaps above all, anger at their own bad luck. The parent's anger is as easy to understand as the child's, different as it is. Unfortunately, understanding falls short even of a first step toward a remedy. All of the energy that goes into this anger must be rerouted toward educated action—patient, unremitting, effective action.

Victor's case is not typical—there is no "typical" learning disabled child—but it is not unusual either. Although caught late, Victor's problems were caught in the nick of time. But let us return to his story.

Victor resented being placed in the special education program, and initially he fell back on his old clowning act. But in the new program, each time he had to be removed from class someone sat down and discussed his behavior with him. The theme was, "You don't like it here, but how are you even going to get back to regular school if you don't stay in class long enough to get the help you need? You're bright, and can overcome your problems, but you can't do that until you're willing to work with us rather than against us." Victor's teacher also tried to point out the probable causes for his misbehavior. When he knocked over his desk, the teacher would say, "I guess it's easier to get mad at the desk than to get mad at yourself because you can't do the math. How about picking up the desk so you can sit down and I can help you?"

I started Victor on a stimulant medication (discussed in Chapter 12). His overactive behavior improved significantly, as did his distractibility. Both his teacher and his family noted a calming effect. His father commented, "Victor went fishing with me and for the first time in his life he quietly sat and enjoyed himself." His mother marveled over a family dinner during which Victor did not jump up and down once. More important, Victor noted a change. He enjoyed the relaxed feeling. He tried to explain the decreased distractibility. "You know what it's like when you are in a room and the refrigerator goes off. Suddenly you realize how much noise it makes. Well, the medicine makes my head quiet. I never realized how much noise was going on up there." And he remained on medication with no objections.

But Victor's general stormy behavior lasted through most of the first year. During this time, Victor was in individual therapy and in family therapy—the therapist saw Victor once a week; the family, every other week. Although Victor had plenty of work to do on his own, most of the effort during the first year went into working with the family. The parents had to regain control both of Victor and of their family life, and, with the therapist's guidance, they established a behavior modification program, including a point system of rewards for Victor and a "time-out" room where he went when things got out of hand. They also had to find ways to recognize and fill their own needs. They had to learn to support each other through the crises with Victor, of course, but they also had to get away for a weekend occasionally, even if they only went to stay with friends in town. As therapy progressed, they learned how to speak candidly and clearly to Victor, reflecting back to him just how he seemed to them and just how they reacted to his behavior, much as his teacher did. In the therapy, Victor's brother also received the support he needed. Encouraged in the belief that Victor had no right to abuse him or to embarrass him in front of his friends, he too learned how to protect his own interests and how to deal more honestly with Victor.

The first year was hard work. Victor made little obvious progress, but everybody felt good about the direction in which they were headed. During the summer, Victor continued in psychotherapy and on the medication.

The first week of the second year in the special school went especially badly. Victor was very angry. He wanted to be back in public school. He could see that he could never make it there, still he just wanted to be there. Then, slowly, he accepted reality. Increasingly he would answer his teacher's reflective comments with "I know! I know!" In therapy, the sad, frightened Victor was most often present. As he struggled with his anger, frustration, and helplessness, he also began to accept the idea that his future was up to him. If he was willing to work, his family and his special education teachers would work just as hard to help him. If he resisted, fought, or played games, his family and teachers would stick by him, but he would not make progress. Frequently, now, he asked to go over the test results again, especially the IQ test. He wondered at times if more medicine would make him better sooner.

Victor began to work at school. He stopped a lot of the clowning behavior. And he learned that he could talk about his feelings rather than act them all out. For example, one afternoon after a very frustrating hour of work on reading, he waited until the rest of the class went to gym, then sat down on the floor near the teacher's desk and cried. His teacher sat still and did nothing. Finally Victor volunteered: "I'm just a retard . . . I'll never learn this stuff. You're wasting your time. My brain is just too dumb to learn." His teacher put his arm around Victor and just listened. Then he told him how glad he was that Victor felt safe enough to share such personal thoughts with him and that he could talk about his feelings rather than acting them out. He also told Victor that the work was indeed hard, but he reassured him that he was bright and would make it.

Victor made up two years of academic work during the second year of the special program. His attitude at home improved, and he formed a good relationship with his father. He returned willingly to the program for the third year, and continued to make progress. At his request, the individual therapy continued.

The next year, Victor returned to his local high school, taking only an hour a day of extra help in the resource room. He continued to need the medication. He completed high school and was accepted in a college that had a special program for students with a history of learning disabilities. He has decided to become a special education teacher. Whatever he does, I have no concerns about Victor's future.

We can never know how much better off Victor might have been had he received earlier—or different—treatment. Perhaps help came at just the moment when he was ready to make use of it. Nor can we know what else Victor's parents might have done earlier or better. Putting ourselves in their place, however, we can certainly suppose that knowing more sooner would have helped them to manage their distressing situation more effectively. The energy they spent doing the best they could might have gone into more productive activities than punishing Victor, punishing the family, and punishing themselves.

If you need not imagine yourself in the shoes of Victor's parents because you are already in them, I shall do the best I can to help you. I wish I could promise to give you a total understanding of the learning disabilities and the other problems associated with them, but I can't. Our field is full of highly trained, concerned, responsible professionals, but we cannot yet account for many of the phenomena we see every day. I can promise you this, however. If partial knowledge is not quite power, it is at least the equipment you must have to fight for the best attention and treatment you can get for your child.

And that is what you must do: fight for the right attention. In a very unusual way, you are a consumer, a consumer of services. These services may not easily be found—they will rarely be thrust at you—but they are there. Your daughter or son will be their most important beneficiary, but you are your child's only agent in this matter. And as your child benefits from the right kind of attention, so do you, and so does your family.

My point is that as soon as you recognize your situation, you must do everything in your power to become an *informed* consumer and an *advocate* for your child. No one and no single agency—not your family physician, not your child's teacher, not the schools, not anyone—is as vitally concerned as you are, or as informed as you can and must be.

A child with learning disabilities confronts a series of Herculean tasks laid out over a long, long course. But the rewards are virtually certain. Your child can improve, can learn to learn, can grow toward becoming a normal, happy adult. That success depends on you— on your action, your assertion, your perseverance, your advocacy. The task of getting help for your child may be smaller than the task facing your child, but it is compelling and it is immediate. It will take all of the strength and determination you have and more. It will baffle, frustrate, and eventually reward you. The task, how- ever, is inescapable, it is imminent, and above all, it is yours alone.

2

Basic Questions and Concepts

To help your daughter or son most effectively, you must have a fair understanding of the child's problems. It may help you, first of all, to realize that 10 to 20 percent of the children in the average school population have trouble with academic work. These youngsters fall into several broad categories: (1) Some are mentally retarded—that is, they have subnormal intellectual capacities, and therefore they will always function below normal levels; (2) some have emotional problems that stand in the way of learning and cause academic difficulties; and (3) some have average or above-average intelligence but still have academic difficulty because of the way their brain or nervous system functions. Although such children may have problems with vision, or hearing, or both, their learning problems are not caused by vision or hearing impairment. The person whom we call "learning disabled" falls into this third group, often called the "neurological group." They represent between 3 and 10 percent of most school populations.

Youngsters with a "neurological" deficit or malfunction usually display a group of problems. Children who have learning disabilities may also be Hyperactive—they cannot sit still and are constantly in motion. They may also be Distractible—every sound, sight, or movement, any event seizes their attention, breaking their concentration and disrupting their thoughts. Children who are hyperactive and/or distractible often have learning disabilities. Most of these youngsters develop emotional, social, and family problems because of the frustrations and failures they experience.

These problems very often occur in the same person. Only rarely does a child have learning disabilities alone. Try to think of the total picture as looking something like this:

1. All of these children have learning disabilities.

2. Many are also Hyperactive and/or Distractible.

3. Almost all develop emotional, social, and family problems.

Let me begin this discussion by answering two preliminary questions that often plague parents confronting treatment of a learning disabled child for the first time: "What do all the terms mean that I hear used to describe my child?" And, "What causes these learning disabilities? Who, or what, is to blame?"

What Do the Terms Applied to My Child Mean?

What shall we call this learning disabled child or adolescent? Everyone seems to have a different name for someone with this group of symptoms. Let us take a quick look at the recent history of our understanding of this problem and review some of the different labels that have been used to describe it.

The research of the 1940s on youngsters with neurologically based learning difficulties suggested that their problems were caused by brain damage. But because these children looked so normal, researchers decided that this brain damage must be very slight. Thus, the earliest label used—and some still use it today—was *Minimal Brain Damage*. Gradually, however, observation and testing revealed that no evidence of damage to the brain could be found in most of these children. In fact, research began to point to the idea that the cause of the problem lay in *how* the brain functions— that is, that it is a physiological problem. All of the brain mechanisms are present and operable, but some of the "wiring" does not work the way it should. Scientists then created a term to suggest this faulty functioning. The prefix *dys-*, which means "difficulty with," was incorporated, and the term *Minimal Brain Dysfunction*, often abbreviated *MBD*, came into use.

During the 1960s and 1970s, professionals in a number of different disciplines studied this problem intensively. Because each discipline trains its specialists and subspecialists differently and uses a different vocabulary to do so, each investigator described what he or she found somewhat differently, much as the blind men did when they studied the elephant. Only now, in the 1980s, are we beginning to see what the whole elephant may look like.

Educators specializing in children with academic problems—the "special education" people—studied these children. Using labels that had been established for many years in schools of education, some saw the various learning disabilities in large categories which covered particular problems. They called trouble with reading *dyslexia*, and the child who had it, dyslexic. The child with writing problems had *dysgraphia* and was called dysgraphic. Trouble with arithmetic they called *dyscalculia*. Other special educators found these terms too general and decided on a terminology which identified learning problems by the specific area of difficulty. Thus, among the *Specific Learning Disabilities* are those involving *perception*, those involving *sequencing*, those involving *memory*, those involving *motor problems*, and those involving *language problems*.

Children who could not keep still or who could not concentrate also came to the attention of physicians and other medical investigators. They called overactive children *hyperactive*, or *hyperkinetic* (*hyper*: over, exceeding; *kinesis*: motion, movement). Children who could not concentrate they labeled *distractible*, or said they were suffering from *Attention Deficit Disorder*.

Many children and adolescents with behavioral difficulties that included learning disabilities were examined by psychiatrists, psychologists, and social workers. The experts in these fields observed that emotional problems could either *cause* a child to have performance problems in school or be a *consequence* of the frustrations and failures that resulted from such performance problems.

Now to return to our question, what shall we call these children and what do the labels mean? Most physicians use the terms *Minimal Brain Dysfunction* or *Attention Deficit Disorder*. Most educators refer to *Specific Learning Disabilities*. The specific labels you see or hear applied to your child reveal the orientation of the person doing the labeling—the field in which she or he was trained and the years during which the person studied learning disabilities in college and graduate school. (Terms in textbooks tend to enjoy a certain currency, then change in favor of newer ones, some more descriptive, some less so.)

The important thing for you to know and remember is that all of these terms refer to the same basic problem in the same one child. Don't let the labels I use here or those that your physician, your child's teacher, or an evaluator uses confuse you. Everyone you consult will want to talk about that aspect of the problem in which he or she specializes. Don't think that the terms they use all refer to different disorders just because someone takes a different approach. All of these terms are simply names for different parts of the same problem. The problem is big enough as it is without compounding it.

What Are the Causes of the Learning Disabilities and Associated Problems?

Before I proceed with my job here—to describe the learning disabilities, their diagnosis, their treatment, and your role in dealing with all of this—I should like to get this question out of the way. Once parents have become aware that they have a learning disabled child or adolescent and have accepted the fact, they immediately ask, "How could this happen? Why did it happen?" as if knowing the cause of something implied knowing its cure. (At the very least, most of us feel better when we have something concrete to blame.)

With regard to the causes of learning disabilities, Hyperactivity, and Distractibility, we simply do not know much. Some research suggests possible chemical imbalances in the brain. Other research attempts to explore broad nutritional issues that may have something to do with these chemical imbalances. But probably there is no one cause. Any number of things, in any number of combinations, could have happened to the nervous system. In most cases, we have no way to reconstruct what actually did happen to a child. I have evaluated children whose histories include major problems during delivery in whom brain damage is quite possible. Yet other children with completely normal deliveries have almost identical disabilities.

I can at least share with you what we do know and what the current state of knowledge suggests about these causes.

Brain Damage

Some learning disabled youngsters may have subtle brain damage. Problems with blood circulation, or with chemicals that do not normally occur in the body, called "toxins," or with chemicals normally in the body but existing at higher or lower levels than normal, called "metabolites," all may affect the developing nervous system of the fetus during pregnancy or at delivery. Certain viral infections may also damage the developing brain. Similar intrusions or accidents may have some impact on the nervous system of the infant during the critical early months or years of life—lead poisoning, for example, or injury, high fever, or certain infections.

A disorder resulting from such a cause may be more or less intense, depending on when in the development of the brain the insult takes place. At one end of the spectrum of consequences is fetal or infant death. In the middle may be cerebral palsy, epilepsy, or mental retardation. The least severe consequence *might be* learning disabilities, Hyperactivity, and Distractibility. But there is no way to predict this, and we cannot often make such an attribution, even after the fact.

Maturational Delay

In some children, the brain matures more slowly than normal. Your child may have experienced a delay in muscle control, in sitting, in standing, or in walking at an age later than normal. Or speech may have been delayed, not starting, perhaps, until age four or five. Or some early infant reflexes, the extension of the arm when the head is turned, or back arching, for example, did not disappear as quickly as they normally should.

Less apparent than muscle control or speech delays are lags in development of auditory perception, visual perception, abstraction ability, memory, and other functions. The brain goes through major growth spurts between three and ten months; between two and four years; between six and eight years; between ten and twelve years; and between fourteen and sixteen years. The brain's final maturation is not completed until one is in one's early thirties. Girls' brains tend to grow and mature more quickly—that is, earlier within these age spans—than boys' brains do. Your child's brain development may simply have slowed down, then leapt forward at some later-than-average age.

Maturational delay can cause learning disabilities with some children. The problem is that the diagnosis is made in retrospect. At this time we can't say that a delay occurred until after it has remedied itself. While the delay exists, the learning disabilities and other undesirable behaviors exist, and the treatment must continue. (It is nice, however, to be the person working with the child when maturation suddenly takes place. Not only do you get the pleasure of seeing the improvement, you get the credit for it too.)

Genetics

Some studies suggest that somewhere between 25 and 40 percent of children and adolescents with learning disabilities have apparently inherited a type of nervous system that is vulnerable to this problem. It tends to run in families: brothers and sisters may have similar difficulties; a mother or father may recall such a problem; an uncle, an aunt, or a cousin may have such a condition. If one of a pair of identical twins has learning problems, the other twin is much more likely to have them than a fraternal twin would be. But we do not know what the genetic code is that might explain this, and we do not know why it is more likely to be passed on to boys than to girls.

Some of the people I have worked with who have had learning disabilities and who have parents or close relatives with the same problems are now young adults. They ask if they should have children, or if they should be careful not to marry someone who has the same problems. I suggest that one usually does not choose whom to fall in love with. I encourage them to have children if they want them but to be very sensitive to their children's preschool and school performance. If their children do have problems, it isn't the worst thing in the world. Help is available.

Although not directly related to a genetic theme, there is another clinical observation that should be noted. The incidence of learning disabilities is four times more common with adopted children than with natural children. We do not know how to explain this. Possibly, mothers who place children for adoption receive less adequate care during pregnancy or have a less adequate diet. We just do not know.

Biochemistry

The brain is made up of millions and millions of nerve cells, each of which has to communicate with other cells. This communication has to take place in such a way that only one other cell, the right cell, is set off. Each cell produces minute amounts of specific chemicals which pass across a microscopic space and stimulate the next, correct cell. These chemicals are called "neurotransmitters" because they transmit messages between nerve cells, or "neurons." Once the jump, called a "synapse," has taken place, another chemical process occurs that breaks down or neutralizes the neurotransmitter.

The brain produces many different types of neurotransmitters. We now know of fifty. We suspect there may be as many as two hundred. Some of the current research suggests that children and adolescents with learning disabilities, Hyperactivity, and/or Distractibility may have a deficiency in one or more of these neurotransmitters or in the breakdown process. Currently the neurotransmitter most frequently being studied is norepinephrine and its breakdown products, dopa and dopamine.

There are other chemical activities and an expanding body of knowledge on these activities. These chemicals control brain and behavioral interactions. New research at the molecular level on the genetic process of transferring messages from the hereditary-carrying gene to the developing brain offers much promise. Specific chemical messengers, called "neuroendocrines," travel to the brain throughout fetal development. Each binds with a particular cell or cell group that has the correct receptor site for this chemical. This binding results in growth of these cells. Each day different sites are stimulated to grow in a very exact and complex process, slowly weaving together the networks of neurons that make up the human brain.

Could these genetic messengers be affected, resulting in a differently wired brain? Could this explain the familial pattern of inheriting learning disabilities? Could certain drugs or other chemicals interfere with the biochemical messenger process, resulting in the absence of brain growth for that particular day or time that the chemical is present? And, would such a block during a brief time impact on other brain growth that should link with this area of nongrowth? Research in molecular genetics and cellular biology offers promise of such answers, and with such answers, hope for prevention or possible treatment concepts.

Lateralization of Brain Function

The adult brain has most functions situated in either the left or the right brain. This lateralization, that is, taking a position on one side or the other, of specialized brain functions begins during fetal growth and continues throughout childhood and beyond. Current research suggests that some children with learning disabilities have altered patterns of lateralization of specific brain functions. But, once again, the applications of this research need further study.

Basic Concepts

Now that you have an idea of what we do *not* know about the causes of learning disabilities and their associated behaviors, you can understand why we cannot yet speak in terms of "prevention" or "cure." We can speak only of "treatment," but it is treatment with a very favorable prognosis. As you go about seeking that treatment for your child, keep these four ideas firmly in mind. You will need them to understand everything that happens to you from now on.

1. Your child is *not* mentally retarded, nor is the child *primarily* emotionally disturbed.

2. Your child probably has a group of difficulties often found together—learning disabilities, Hyperactivity, Distractibility, and emotional, social, and family problems. Know which ones your son or daughter has.

3. These disabilities are not just school problems. They interfere with every aspect of your child's life—at home, with friends, in sports, in activities. You must learn to understand every aspect of your youngster's disabilities and how they affect him or her in all these aspects, as well as how they affect you and the members of your family.

4. You must learn to build on strengths while understanding and compensating for weaknesses. If possible, never magnify weaknesses.

Your child's problems may seem overwhelming. But keep in mind what I just said in another context. Although this condition is unfortunate, it is not the worst thing in the world. Many, many people can help you understand more, not only about your situation and that of your child, but about what remedies will work. You must know as much as possible about what to ask, who to ask, and what to demand. The people you meet will help you to learn more about what they can do and about what your child can do. Only you are motivated enough to push for appropriate testing and constructive remedies. Only you know your child well enough to see that he or she gets the best help you can find.

3

The Specific Learning Disabilities

All of us have areas in which we learn very readily. A few of us even seem to excel in limited areas with very little apparent learning: thus, the "natural" athlete, the musical "genius," the "gifted" artist. All of us also have areas in which our abilities will never be more than average, and a few areas in which we cannot seem to learn anything. The youngster with learning disabilities has areas of strength and of average ability too. This child, however, has larger areas, or different areas, of learning weaknesses than most people do. Each person displays a different pattern of strengths and weaknesses. You must learn as much as you can about the whole pattern that your child displays, the disabilities, of course, but also the abilities. What your child *can* do, and may indeed do well, is just as important as what she or he cannot do because that is what you have to build on.

You may have suspected a learning disability before your child entered school. This concern became real when he or she failed to learn the skills being taught.

He or she may have read letters backwards or confused certain letters. Or he or she may have misunderstood what you said or have been slow in developing speech or muscle coordination.

In order to talk a little more usefully about learning disabilities, let me quickly outline a simple scheme describing what the brain must do in order for learning to take place. The first step is *input*, getting information into the brain from the eyes, the ears, the nose, the mouth, and special nerve endings in the skin and muscles. Once this information has arrived, the brain needs to make sense out of it, a process called *integration*. Next, the information must be stored and later retrieved, the *memory* process. Finally, the brain must send some kind of message back to the nerves and muscles—its *output*.

The brain does a great deal more than this, of course, much of which we understand little about. But this simplified scheme will do for our purposes. Once again, then, the learning processes are:

Input
Integration
Memory
Output

Input Disabilities

Information arrives at the brain as impulses, transmitted along neurons, primarily from our eyes—called "visual input"—and from our ears—called "auditory input." This input process takes place in the brain. It does not pertain to visual problems, such as near-sightedness or farsightedness, or to any hearing problems. This central input process of seeing, or hearing, or in any other way taking in or perceiving one's environment is referred to as "perception." Thus we speak of a child who has a perceptual disability in the area of visual input as having a *visual perceptual disability*, and one with a disability in the area of auditory input as having an *auditory perceptual disability*. Some children have *both* kinds of perceptual disability, or they may have problems when both inputs are needed *at the same time*—for example, seeing what the teacher writes on the blackboard while listening to the explanation of what is being written.

Visual Perceptual Disabilities

Your child may have difficulty in organizing the position and shape of what he or she sees. Input may be perceived with letters reversed or rotated: An *e* might look like an ℮; and *E* might look like a *W*, or a *3*, or an *M*. The child may confuse similar looking letters because of these rotations or reversals: *d*, *b*, *p*, *g*, and *q* may be confused with any one of the others. The word *was* might be perceived as *saw*, or *dog* as *god*. This confusion with position of input shows up almost immediately when the child begins to read, to write, or to copy letters or designs.

Another child might have a "figure-ground" problem, that is difficulty in focusing on the significant figure instead of all the other visual inputs in the background. This occurs in real-life situations as well as in looking at printed matter or electronic images. For example, the child is told to pass the salt shaker but has difficulty finding it among the many dishes and platters. Reading requires focusing on specific letters or groups of letters, then tracking from left to right, line after line. Children with this disability may have reading problems. They jump over words or skip lines.

Judging distance is another visual perceptual task which can go awry. Your child may misjudge depth, bumping into things, falling off a chair, or knocking over a drink because the hand reaches too far for it. What you take for habitual carelessness or poor eyesight may in fact be just this sort of perceptual error.

There are other types of visual perceptual problems. While playing in an open field or gym, your child may become confused and disoriented because of trouble organizing his or her position in space. Or the child may have difficulty in understanding left and right, or up and down.

One very common type of visual perceptual disability relates to doing things when the eyes have to tell the hands or legs what to do. When such information is unreliable, activities like catching a ball, jumping rope, doing puzzles, or using a hammer and nails become difficult or impossible. To catch a ball, the eyes must focus on the ball (figure-ground), the brain must perceive the correct position and path of the ball (depth perception) and tell the various parts of the body exactly where to move and when, and then the body must obey. A child who misperceives distance or speed, or whose brain misdirects the body, will miss the ball completely.

Auditory Perceptual Disabilities

As with visual perception, your child may have difficulty with one or several aspects of auditory perception. Those who have difficulty distinguishing subtle differences in sounds will misunderstand what you are saying and respond incorrectly. Words that sound alike are often confused—"blue" and "blow," or "ball" and "bell." I once asked a child, "How are you?" He answered, "I'm nine." He thought he heard an "old" instead of "are," or in addition to the "are."

Some children have difficulty with auditory figure-ground. He or she might be watching television in a room where others are playing or talking. You are in the kitchen and call out to the child. You might be into your third paragraph before he or she begins to pick your voice (figure) out of the other sound inputs (background). It appears that the child never listens or pays attention.

I recall observing Mary in her fourth grade classroom. She had been evaluated and found to have learning disabilities, one of which was an auditory figure-ground problem. She later helped me understand what I observed, but let me tell the story as it happened. She was at her desk reading a story. Other children were talking in the back of the room; there was the noise of movement in the hall and traffic outside. The teacher suddenly said, "Children, let's do math. Open up your book to page 38 and try problem five." Mary looked over and saw her friend take out her math book. So, she did the same. She then looked over the shoulder of the boy in front of her to see what page he was on. At this moment the teacher shouted, "Mary, stop bothering John and get to work." She then looked at me sitting in the back of the room and said, "See what I mean." Mary was confused and hurt because she did not know what she had done wrong. Of course, by the time Mary realized that the teacher was speaking she only heard "and try problem five." But the teacher was frustrated because she did not know of Mary's disabilities.

Some children cannot process sound inputs as fast as normal people can. This is called an "auditory lag." If you speak at a normal pace, the child may miss part of what you are saying. You have to speak slower, or give separate instructions, before he or she can follow you. If you were to say, "It's getting late—go upstairs, wash your face and get into your pajamas, then come down for a snack," your child may hear only the first part and stay upstairs. If you gave the first part of the instructions, then waited a few seconds before you added the rest, however, the child might hear the whole thing.

Disabilities with Input from the Other Senses

Some children appear to be unable to understand tactile input or touch fully and appear to dislike being touched. Children who are clumsy may be having difficulty with messages coming into the brain from certain nerve endings in the muscles (called "proprioceptors"). At this time we know very little about such perceptual disabilities. Future studies should help us to understand them better. We also have to wait for future studies for more knowledge of smell and taste disabilities.

Integration Disabilities

Once the information coming into the brain is registered, it has to be understood. At least two steps are required to do this: sequencing and abstraction.

Suppose that your brain recorded the following three graphic symbols: a *d*, an *o*, and a *g*. No problem with visual perception. But to make sense of the perception, you have to place the symbols in the right order, or sequence. Is it *d-o-g*, or *g-o-d* or *d-g-o*, or what? Then you have to infer meaning from the context in which the word is used, both a general meaning and a specific meaning. For example, *the dog* and *you dog* have very different meanings. The ability to draw general applications from specific words and to attach subtle shadings to the basic meanings of words is referred to as "abstract thinking."

The process of integrating input, of understanding what your brain has recorded, thus requires both *sequencing* and *abstraction*. Your child might have a disability in one area or the other, or both. A child who has difficulty sequencing what comes in from the eyes is said to have a *visual sequencing disability*. If the difficulty lies with what comes in through the ears, it is called an *auditory sequencing disability*. So too, the child might have difficulty with *visual abstraction* and *auditory abstraction*.

Sequencing Disabilities

A child with such a disability might hear or read a story, but, in recounting it, start in the middle, go to the beginning, then shift to the end. Eventually the whole story comes out, but the sequence of events is wrong. Or a child might see the math problem as $16-3=$? on the blackboard but write it as $61-3=$? Or a child might see $2+3=$? and write $2+5=3$. The child knows the right answer but gets the sequence wrong. Spelling words with all of the right letters in the wrong order can also reflect this disability.

Or a child may memorize a sequence—the days of the week, for example—and then be unable to use single units out of that sequence correctly. If you ask what comes after Wednesday, the child cannot answer spontaneously but must go back over the whole list, "Sunday, Monday, Tuesday, Wednesday . . .," before she or he can answer.

A child with a sequence disability might hit the baseball then run to third rather than first base or have difficulty with board games that require moving in a particular sequence. Or when setting the dinner table he or she might have trouble placing each item in the proper place.

Abstraction Disabilities

Once information is recorded in the brain and placed in the right sequence, one must be able to infer meaning. Most learning disabled children have only minor difficulties in this area. Abstraction—the ability to derive the correct general meaning from a particular word or symbol—is a very basic intellectual task. If the disability in this area is too great, the child is apt to be functioning at a retarded level.

Some children do, however, have problems with abstraction. The teacher may be doing a language-arts exercise with a group of second-graders. He or she reads a story about a police officer, let us say. The teacher then begins a discussion of police officers in general, asking the pupils if they know any men or women who are police officers in their neighborhoods, and, if so, what do they do? A child with an abstraction disability may not be able to answer such a question. He or she can only talk about the particular officer in the story and not about law officers in general.

Memory Disabilities

Once information is received, recorded in the brain, and integrated, it has to be stored so that it can be retrieved later. This storage-

and-retrieval process we call memory, and there are two types: short-term memory and long-term memory.

Short-term memory is the process by which you hold on to information as long as you are concentrating on it. For example, when you call the information operator for a long-distance number, you get a ten-digit number with an area code. Like most people, you can probably retain these numbers long enough to dial the number if you do it right away and nothing interrupts your attention. However, if someone starts talking to you in the course of dialing, you may lose the number. Or, you might go to the store with five things in mind to buy, but by the time you get there so many different impressions have intervened that you've forgotten an item or two on your list.

Long-term memory refers to the process by which you store information that you have repeated often enough. You can retrieve this information quickly by thinking of it—you can come up with your current home address and phone number quite readily, for example—or you may have to spend a little more time and effort to think of it—your mother's home address, for example.

If your child has a memory disability, it is most likely a short-term one. Like abstraction disabilities, long-term memory disabilities interfere so much with functioning that children who have them are more likely to be classified as retarded. It may take ten to fifteen repetitions for a child with this problem to retain what the average child retains after three to five repetitions. Yet the same child usually has no problem with long-term memory. Your child probably surprises you at times by coming up with details that you have forgotten about something that happened several years ago.

A short-term memory disability can occur with information learned through what one sees—*visual short-term memory disability*—or with information learned through what one hears—*auditory short-term memory disability*. Often the two are combined. For example, you might go over a spelling list one evening with your son. He looks at it several times, listens to you, and can write down the spellings correctly from memory. He seems to have it down pat, but that's because he's concentrating on it. The next morning he has lost most or all of the words. Or a teacher may go over a math concept in class until your daughter understands it—she's concentrating on it. Yet when she comes home that night and does her homework, she has completely forgotten how to do the problems.

David was fifteen when I first started working with him. He

had been known to have learning disabilities and had been in special education classes. He was now in regular classes and doing poorly with peers. During the early sessions he would begin to tell me something, then say, "Oh, forget it" and stop. His parents had reported this behavior at home, and it made them angry with him. Finally, I asked David to help me understand this response. He could not. I then told him that I knew he had a memory problem and wondered if this had anything to do with it. He looked embarrassed as he explained that sometimes he started to say something then, "half way through the paragraph I forget where I started or what I meant to say. I get so mad at myself I just say forget it." This often happened when he was with friends, too, and much of the time he just kept quiet rather than risk "looking like a fool."

Output Disabilities

Information comes out of the brain either by means of words—language output—or through muscle activity, such as writing, drawing, gesturing, and so forth—motor output. A child or adolescent may have a *language disability* or a *motor disability*.

Language Disability

Two forms of language are used in communication, spontaneous language and demand language. You use *spontaneous language* in situations where you initiate whatever is said. Here you have the luxury of picking the subject and taking some time to organize your thoughts and to find the correct words before you say anything. In a *demand language* situation, someone else sets up a circumstance in which you must communicate. A question is put to you, for example. Now you have no time to organize your thoughts or find the right words; you have only a split second in which you must simultaneously organize, find words, and answer more or less appropriately.

Children with a *specific language disability* usually have no difficulty with spontaneous language. They do, however, often have problems with demand language. The inconsistency can be quite striking. A youngster may initiate all sorts of conversation, may never keep quiet, in fact, and may sound quite normal. But put into a situation that demands a response, the same child might answer "Huh?" or "What?" or "I don't know." Or the child may ask you to repeat the question to gain time, or not answer at all. If the child is forced to answer, the response may be so confusing or circumstantial that it is difficult to follow. She or he may sound totally unlike the child who was speaking so fluently just a minute ago. This inconsistency or confusion in language behavior often puzzles parents and teachers. A teacher might put a child down as lazy or negative because he or she does well when volunteering to speak or answer a question, but won't answer or says "I don't know" when called on. The explanation could lie in the child's inability to handle demand language, but contradictory behavior like this makes sense only if you know about the disability.

Motor Disabilities

If a child has difficulty in using large muscle groups, this is called a *gross motor disability*. Difficulty in performing tasks that require many muscles to work together in an integrated way is called a *fine motor disability*.

Gross motor disabilities may cause your child to be clumsy, to stumble, to fall, to bump into things, or to have trouble with generalized physical activities like running, climbing, or swimming.

The most common form of fine motor disability shows up when the child begins to write. The problem lies in an inability to get the many muscles in the dominant hand to work together as a team. Children and adolescents with this "written language" disability have slow and poor handwriting. A typical expression of this problem is, "My hand doesn't work as fast as my head is thinking."

Watch your own hand as you write something and notice the many detailed fine muscle activities that it takes to write legibly. Writing requires a constant flow of such activities. Now place your pen in your nondominant hand and try to write. If you go very slowly, it is tedious but your handwriting is legible. If you go at a regular pace, however, your hand aches and your handwriting deteriorates immediately. Shape, size, spacing, positioning—everything about it looks awful no matter how hard you try. A child with a fine motor disability goes through this all the time.

When a child has a visual perceptual problem, the brain, which has incorrectly recorded or processed information, will probably misinform the muscles during activities that require eye-hand coordination. We have already touched on these *visual motor disabilities* in the section on Visual Perceptual Disabilities.

Jill, a high-school junior, illustrates this problem. She was bright but had learning disabilities. Her written language disability was a great frustration. Her hand just did not work as fast as her brain. "When I have to write something in class or take an essay exam, I have two choices. I either slow my thoughts down to the speed my hand writes and don't finish or I speed my hand up to keep up with my thoughts but write so poorly that the teacher marks me down or I make silly spelling and grammar errors." Jill had difficulty with multiple-choice exams, especially when there was a separate answer sheet where you have to mark the right space. She would mark the wrong space or skip a line, and then the computer marked all of the remaining answers wrong. She learned to compensate by stopping after each ten or so questions and checking that she marked the correct spot. This took time, however, and she once moaned, "I wish school would grade me on what I know rather than what I can put on a piece of paper."

Establishing Your Child's Profile

Obviously the learning process is much more complex, but this simple model for describing specific learning disabilities should be helpful. The important thing is that if your child has one or more of these disabilities, you must know that, along with your son's or daughter's specific profile of strengths and weaknesses.

Look at the checklist of specific learning disabilities below. Do you know where your child's disabilities lie? Where the strengths lie? If not, ask the special-education team at your school or the person who does the testing to clarify this for you.

Specific Learning Disabilities

Input
  Visual perception
  Auditory perception
Integration
  Visual sequencing
  Auditory sequencing
  Visual abstraction
  Auditory abstraction
Memory
  Visual short-term memory

Auditory short-term memory
Visual long-term memory
Auditory long-term memory
Output
Spontaneous language
Demand language
Gross motor
Fine motor

4

Hyperactivity, Distractibility with a Short Attention Span, and Other Problems

We have already noted that the term "Hyperactivity" refers to the child or adolescent who cannot sit still, who appears always to be moving. "Distractibility" refers to the person whose attention is so easily caught by sights, sounds, movements, or any other event, that he or she cannot concentrate on anything for any length of time. Children with learning disabilities are not all Hyperactive and/or Distractible—research studies suggest that the number is about 25 percent. Most who are Hyperactive and/or Distractible— about 85 percent—do turn out to have learning disabilities, however.

Hyperactivity

Not all overactive children are Hyperactive, and the distinction between neurologically based and any other kind of overactivity is extremely important. The term "Hyperactive" is applied very loosely these days to too many children whom it does not describe. In this book, I use "Hyperactive" to refer exclusively to that neurologically based behavior so often associated with learning disabilities, and I use a capital "H" to emphasize the distinction. (The same is true for Distractibility.)

A child or adolescent can be overactive for a number of reasons. The most common cause of such behavior is anxiety. We are all more restless when we are upset and anxious about something. Children, especially, frequently relieve their anxieties by increased muscle activity. Depression can also cause overactivity. Although depression often shows itself in quietness, withdrawal from people, and isolation, it may also appear as irritability, snapping at people, and bursts of temper. Children who express their depression this latter way may appear to be hyperactive.

The least common cause of overactive behavior, but the only kind that concerns us here, appears to be due to a specific nervous system difficulty in which an imbalance may exist between the part of the brain that stimulates muscle activity and the part of the brain that decreases it. This neurologically based Hyperactivity is the kind that shows up in some children who have learning disabilities.

A careful look at the history of your child's behavior should give you a useful clue to the cause of the overactivity. If the behavior occurs only at certain times or in certain places, or if specific experiences seem to cause it, it is probably due to anxiety. For example, if your child is overactive only at school, or if the child was never overactive until a certain grade, or if he or she is overactive only when you are arguing with someone, the problem is anxiety-based. If the overactivity began after a stressful experience—the birth of a sibling, a divorce, the death of a family member—you might consider depression as the cause.

But if the overactive behavior has been present ever since the child was born, it is probably neurologically based Hyperactivity. The child may even have moved around more and kicked more before it was born. Always in motion, rarely sitting still, the baby squirmed in your arms, rolled in the crib, ran as soon as she or he walked. The Hyperactivity occurs generally, with no relation to specific events. Not limited to school or any other hours, it occurs all the time and any place.

About 85 percent of Hyperactive children grow out of this behavior as they mature during puberty. Fifteen to 20 percent may remain Hyperactive through adolescence and possibly young adulthood, however. (We go into this prospect and what to do about it in the chapters on treatment.)

Distractibility

Distractible behavior also has several causes. Anxiety can cause distractibility. When you are anxious, it is hard to concentrate. Depression, especially when expressed as withdrawal, can seem to be Distractibility. When you are depressed and withdrawn, it is difficult to focus on anything.

The least common cause of distractible behavior appears to be a specific nervous system difficulty in which the brain does not adequately filter out sensory inputs. We continually receive inputs from all of our senses. Normally we filter out unimportant stimuli and pay attention only to those that are important. The less important inputs are not blocked out, however; they are simply monitored at a lower level of consciousness in the brain and never come into sharp focus. For example, you may get in your car and drive home, then realize that you were so busy thinking that you don't know how you got there. Those inputs that you had to notice—steering, brake lights, landmarks, traffic signals—were relayed to the brain and responded to, but you may have been thinking or daydreaming about many other things. Or, at the playground, you hear a number of children calling "Mommy" or "Daddy," yet you *hear* only your child's voice.

Some children and adolescents have "filter systems" that function poorly. Every input passes to the higher levels of the brain and demands attention. Some are more distracted by visual phenomena than by auditory ones; some are just the reverse. But because of this Distractibility, all have short attention spans.

Just as with Hyperactive behavior, the child's history should indicate the probable cause of Distractible behavior. If the attention problem occurs only at certain times or places or in conjunction only with certain events, think of anxiety. If it occurs after a stressful experience, think of depression. However, if the Distractibility and short attention-span have been present throughout the child's life, it is probably neurologically based.

As with Hyperactivity, about 85 percent of neurologically Distractible children grow out of it during puberty, while 15 to 20 percent remain Distractible through adolescence and possibly young adulthood. (Again, I talk about treatment in later chapters.)

Other Neurological and Behavior Problems

In addition to the learning disabilities and possibly Hyperactivity and Distractibility, your daughter or son may display other problem behaviors, among them (1) perseveration, (2) persisting immature reflexes and other signs of an immature nervous system, and (3) impulsivity. You may also note certain physical differences in your infant. None of these is *necessarily* associated with learning disabilities. Still, they may occur in your son or daughter, and we should look at them briefly. Each is another reflection of a central nervous system difficulty.

Perseveration ⭒ *especially when desires something*

At times your child may repeat a word or a phrase over and over, *crying* or ask the same question repeatedly, or start an activity and persist in it beyond the bounds of good sense. Repetitive behavior like this may be another evidence of abnormal brain activity. It is as if the circuits jam. The youngster lines up cars or soldiers, for example, then keeps on lining them up without apparent purpose, or starts talking about something or asking a question and cannot get off it and onto another topic.

We do not understand this behavior, nor do we have a treatment for it. The best approach is a very practical one, although not always an easy one. Try to help the child break the pattern. With activities, you might put away the objects the child is using. With questions, you may have to say that you will not answer any more of them, then try to ignore them or walk away.

Persisting Immature Reflexes and Other Signs
of an Immature Nervous System

During the first four months of life, certain automatic body responses, or "reflexes," usually disappear. These reflexes are normal in a newborn infant, but as the brain matures, it suppresses or controls these behaviors. For some children who will turn out to have learning disabilities, these reflexes persist longer than normal. They may also persist in babies who will *not* be learning disabled, however, so don't take this as a sign, simply as a possible clue.

These reflexes can interfere with your feeding and holding the baby, and if this happened it may have created ambivalent feelings in you and frustrations in your infant. Although it is too late now to offer help, if you can look back and understand your feelings, you may be able to think about that time a little more realistically and feel less anxious and guilty.

One such reflex is called the "tonic-neck reflex." When you turn your infant's head to one side, the arm on that side automatically extends and moves out, while the arm on the other side bends, going up over the head. This reflex is present at two weeks of age, peaks at about two months, then declines, often disappearing completely by sixteen weeks. If it persisted in your child, you may have noticed that when you held your infant and turned its head toward the bottle or the nipple, its arm moved out as if to push you away.

Another persistent reflex relates to a reflex which is characteristic of young infants. When muscles are stretched, they reflexively contract. This is called a "stretch reflex." As you held your infant to feed it, for example, you may have noticed that when you put your finger in the infant's hand, its fingers closed over your finger. Another stretch reflex occurs when the pressure of your upper arm against the baby's back causes the back muscles to contract—that is, it arches its back. If both the "back-arching reflex" and the "tonic-neck reflex" are present, when you pick up your infant, place it in your arm, and turn its face toward you, the baby seems to "back off" and "push you away," almost as if it were rejecting you. Perhaps these behaviors were the earliest examples of your child's "invisible" disability which were not understood and which resulted in a conflict in relating. The consequence may be poor interaction with the people who are most important and necessary to the baby—you, the parents.

A third suggestion of immature reflexes occurs when the startle reaction persists. Normally, if an infant's head is lowered or dropped quickly, it will startle—the back extends, the arms extend and move out, the hands and fingers are held wide open. The legs may do the same. This reflex usually disappears by three to four months. If it continues beyond this time, it may be another evidence of neurological problems.

Hypersensitivity to touch can be another possible evidence of an immature nervous system during early infancy. Some infants perceive touch as unpleasant or painful. They appear to be tactilely defensive. When a parent holds such a baby, it cries. The more you try to comfort it by holding it tighter or cuddling it, the more it cries. Some parents report that they intuitively learned to place their baby on a pillow and then hold the pillow, or to place it on the bed and prop up the bottle beside it.

Such hypersensitivity is often suppressed by the fifth or sixth week of life. Some cases of "milk allergies" may instead be cases of skin hypersensitivity. It is not that a change in milk at six or seven weeks finally works. Rather, the hypersensitivity stops at that age, and the child can relax. Any milk given at this time will work.

Some infants seem more irritable and active than normal. It is as if the nervous system is easily upset, and any activity, sound, or movement can produce shaking or crying. We suspect that this too, reflects an immature nervous system which cannot maintain an even balance.

Motor disabilities may also be present early. Poor coordination of muscles in the tongue, cheeks, lips, and throat can cause eating and swallowing problems. The baby uses the same muscles to eat as to swallow, and if the baby swallows poorly, saliva builds up, causing excessive drooling.

Note once again that none of these problems have any necessary correlation with learning disabilities. But to the degree that they do coexist, and because they constitute problems in and of themselves as well as occasionally indicating other conditions, you should be aware of them and of what they may possibly mean.

Impulsivity

As a child gets older, he or she learns to wait for longer periods of time between the impulse to act or react and the actual action or reaction. This delay gives the child some time to consider all of the possible responses she or he might make, to recall similar past experiences, and to think about the consequences of an action.

Some learning disabled children and adolescents do not have this ability to delay between impulse and response. They act immediately, without apparent thought. In terms of behavior, they appear never to learn from experience—they can't wait long enough to recall past experience. They act before they think. The result is apparent misbehavior such as hitting, or knocking things over. For some, this reflects emotional immaturity; for others, it may be evidence of an immature nervous system.

Impulsive children may also have other difficulties. Some have trouble with bladder control beyond the usual age of two or three years. When the impulse from the bladder to say it is full reaches the brain, the brain can usually send back a signal to hold on until reaching a bathroom. For some, this delay is not possible. Such children may be chronic bedwetters. An immature nervous system, emotional problems, or physical problems—or a combination of any of these—may be the reason. You should start your investigation into the causes of such conditions by consulting the child's physician.

Impulsive children may also become preoccupied with playing with matches, setting fires, or stealing, for example. If your child develops any of these antisocial and dangerous behaviors, you should discuss them with a mental health professional.

Physical Differences

Some children show slight variations in the physical characteristics that we consider "normal." The ears may be set slightly lower or higher on the head. The eyes may be a little farther apart or closer together. Certain fingers or toes may be longer or shorter. None of these variations should alarm you. No definite correlation has been found between any such physical features and learning disabilities. However, children with learning disabilities have a higher likelihood of such differences than normal children.

Understanding Your Child's Profile

In the previous chapter I described the types of specific learning disabilities your child might have. In this chapter I have described other neurologically based behaviors that may be present in children with learning disabilities:

- Hyperactivity
- Distractibility
- Perseveration
- Persistent Immature Reflexes
- Tactile Defensiveness
- Impulsivity

Know which of these behaviors, if any, your child or adolescent has. If you suspect that one of these problems was or is present, or if you are unsure, discuss your observations with your family physician.

Part Two

Problems in Psychological, Emotional, and Social Development

5

Normal Psychosocial Development

A mother called me about her child. Her son refuses to leave her, she said, clinging and crying if she tries to walk away. If she leaves him with someone else, he throws a tantrum. What should she do with him? I couldn't say anything until I found out her son's age. If he were one year old, this could be quite normal. If he were two, I would be slightly worried. If he were four or eight, I would be very concerned. If he were fifteen, I would be alarmed. "Normal" behavior has a great deal to do with your son's or daughter's age and the stage of development the child is in at the time.

All children go through stages of psychological and social development, and most do so with minimal difficulty. They may occasionally face a stressful situation—being in the hospital, or getting used to a new baby brother or sister, or coping with their parents' divorce—and briefly retreat back to earlier behaviors. But ordinarily they soon rally and move ahead again. Growth means many steps forward with occasional steps backward.

Much of this psychological and social—psychosocial—growth interweaves with stages in physical growth. As the brain and body mature, the child develops new abilities with which to handle problems. This same growth, however, also introduces new problems.

Many children go through the various stages of development noticeably, but without serious problems. Most children go through these stages with few obvious difficulties. Some children and families find certain stages of growth more difficult than others. The child with a learning disability, however, may have trouble with some or all stages of psychosocial development. But we must first review what we understand to be normal development before we can go into the ways in which learning disabilities inhibit or alter this development.

Normal Child Development

The newborn infant functions primarily as a physiological being, the brain receiving messages from the body and sending out messages to the body to respond. During the early weeks and months, the baby begins to become conscious of certain significant people, recognizing mother's or father's voice, image, or smell, for example. As the infant begins to relate to its world, it is unaware of any distinction between its body and things in the environment, it has no sense of any boundaries. People, pets, food, furniture, favorite toys—all objects outside of the self appear to be merely extensions of the self. For now, the infant and its world are one.

This stage of development looks something like this.

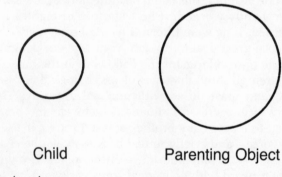

Child   Parenting Object

Basic trust

Gradually the infant begins to discover that things have extensions and limits to them as well. It discovers its fingers, and hands, toes,and feet, and finds that these objects belong to the same body that it has begun to experience. By three months the infant can recognize certain pieces of the external world, and it relates to these "part objects" in special ways which acknowledge their importance. Now we see for the first time the "social smile"—the child looks at a part of a face and smiles. This social smile is an early psychological landmark of normal development.

By nine months, most infants have completed the process of discovering where they leave off and the world begins. They have discovered that there are many human objects in the world. Having learned to associate pleasurable experiences with certain human objects, the baby begins to comprehend that these specific human objects are very important—that they are absolutely necessary, in fact. Thus the baby learns to place a *basic trust* in these key people, and it becomes *totally dependent* on them

With the establishment of basic trust, the infant masters the first major step in psychosocial development. But now the baby becomes upset if it is left alone. It fears separation and it fears strangers. Before this stage, anyone could pick up the baby and get a smile. Now if someone unknown, or not very well-known, picks up the baby, it starts to cry. This fear, which normally appears at around nine months, is another psychological landmark.

This stage of total dependency might look like this.

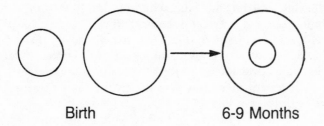

<table>
<tr><td>Birth</td><td>6-9 Months</td></tr>
</table>

Separation

The next task in psychosocial development is *separation*. The infant must realize that it can separate from these significant people and still survive, and then learn how to do that. Mastery of this stage of development involves several steps which start at about nine to twelve months and usually finish at three to three-and-one-half years. This accomplishment of separation, which leads to a sense of an autonomous self, is illustrated in the figure below.

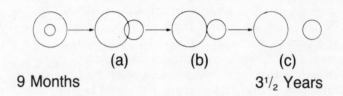

(a)   (b)   (c)

9 Months   3¹/₂ Years

Initially (see A in the figure), the infant must have some form of sensory connection with the significant person. The baby cries, hears a parent's footsteps in the hall, and stops crying. This auditory linkage is enough. Or the infant crawls behind a chair, loses sight of a parent, and cries. When the parent moves into view, it stops. This visual link, the sight of the parent, reestablishes the necessary contact. The baby cries at night. When the mother or father pick it up in the dark and hold it, it stops crying. The touch, smell, and voice of the parent reassure the infant that the intimate connection is not broken.

Beginning at about eighteen to twenty-four months, the child slowly learns to separate for longer and longer periods of time (see B in the figure). Yet the toddler still must return frequently to the parent to "refuel" or "tag up." A hug or a kiss or a cookie will do, and the child is off again. Some children find these early efforts at separating easier if they can take something that reminds them of a parent along with them. Children usually select these favorite things, which we commonly call "security blankets" but more properly call "transitional objects," because they have a familiar smell, soft touch, or cuddly feel which they have learned to associate with the parent.

By about three to three-and-a-half years, the child can finally separate from his or her parents with no discomfort (see C in the figure). This full mastery of separation is yet another landmark in development.

Two major psychological events take place during this stage, one internally motivated, the other, externally caused. Each aids in mastering separation and in establishing autonomy, and each has a major influence on personality development. The internal event is *negativism*, and this begins at about age two. During the "terrible twos," the child responds to most requests or comments with "No," or "No, I do myself." The child is beginning to separate and to show that he or she has a mind of his own. Although exasperating to parents, this healthy step toward separation and autonomy is a very necessary one.

The other event which occurs at about age two is *toilet training*. In learning to accede to this requirement of the outside world, the child confronts two new concepts which have to be mastered. First, the child must alter his or her concept of love and relationships. Until now the child has perceived the whole world as being there to take care of her or him. Love and caring were automatic and free. Suddenly the child faces a situation in which love is no longer free and available on demand. Now if the child wants love, he or she must do something to get it. Loving relationships no longer center totally around one's wishes and needs; now the child must learn to participate in a give-and-take process. Urinate in the potty and mommy loves you; urinate in your pants and mommy frowns or spanks or threatens not to love you. Getting love sometimes requires doing what is wanted—that is, what is lovable. To receive pleasure requires pleasing. This forces the child to make a revolutionary shift in her or his concept of the world, of people, and of relationships.

Toilet training introduces a second new concept which provides the child with a new way to handle angry feelings. For the first time the child has an active weapon in the battle to get what he or she wants. Prior to this, the child could cry or have a tantrum, but the parents could choose to ignore it. Prior to this, the child experienced anger and expressed it openly by crying, screaming, kicking, or hitting. Now the child begins to realize that there are different ways to express anger, and that the way one does express anger has a great deal to do with getting and keeping love. Direct expressions of anger don't work—the price one has to pay may be too great. Children now learn that more indirect expressions of anger work somewhat better than hitting and yelling. Now when angry with a parent they can squat right in front of them, preferably when company is around, and, with a big smile, "make" in their pants. If they are pleased with mommy and daddy, they will "make" on the potty. The child begins to learn the importance of controlling anger, or more precisely, of learning subtler, more ambiguous, and therefore more acceptable ways to express anger.

These issues—the reciprocal nature of loving and being loved and pleasing and being pleased, and handling angry feelings—are struggled with individually and together. The two themes often interrelate: at this age one can readily love and hate the same person at the same time or hurt and care for the same person at the same time.

Individuation

When the child has mastered the first major task of development, establishing basic trust, and the second major task, handling separation, he or she is ready for the third task, *individuation*. This task involves asking and trying to answer the question "Who am I?" Now that the child knows that he or she is a separate person who can survive without being totally dependent on important people, what kind of person is that child? The struggle to answer these questions usually takes place between the ages of three and six.

At this age, the brain is still immature, and not all thinking is based on reality. Fantasy, which seems as real as what is real, forms one basis for a lot of the thinking a child does. If one thinks something is so, it may as well be so. Children at this age, then, can have opposite beliefs and feelings simultaneously, with no notion that a contradiction exists, or that only one of two or more different possibilities can come true. Loving and hating, wanting and not wanting, going to a movie and at the same time going on a picnic—the child excludes nothing and sees no problem with believing in all possibilities coming true at the same time.

Children also try out many roles. If the child pretends to be Superman, she or he *is* Superman. What is it like to be big? Little? Aggressive? Submissive? A boy? A girl? Children play "house" or "school" or "doctor," exploring various roles and different situations. One day your daughter may be a boy, the next day a girl, or a mommy, a daddy, a teacher, a gangster, ET, or Miss Piggy. Your daughter or son tries to learn about people and how to do things and tries to master those concerns through repetition in play. For example, children must learn to listen to adults other than their parents. When they play school, they take turns being the teacher who gives instructions and orders and then the pupil who must listen and obey. When they play doctor, they take turns being the doctor who explores and the patient who is explored.

Whenever a child tries to "be" someone else in the family, mother or father, for instance, he or she has to compete with that person for her or his identity as well as with any sibling who may also want to be that parent. The child also has to try to attract the attention of the other parent. So another characteristic of this age period is the child's tendency to cause splitting and tension be

tween parents as well as among siblings. Children learn with re-
markable aptitude how to divide parents, getting one closer to them
and pushing the other away. Thus, on one day a child may seem
close and loving, yet on another day he or she is irritating and
hostile.

For the first item, in the figure below, our diagram of the child's
relationships must include both parents.

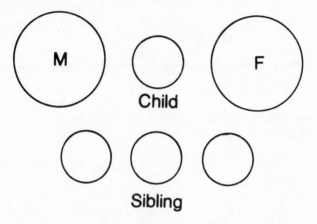

If the boy or girl wants to play "being mother," then mother
must be pushed away, along with any siblings who might compete
for her role, as in the figure below.

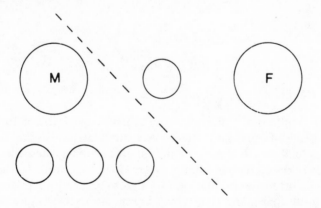

If the child wants to play "being father," then father has to be
pushed away, along with any siblings who might want *that* role,
as in the figure that follows.

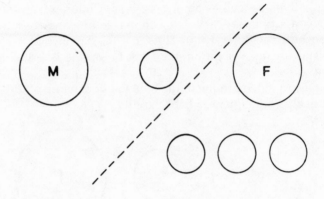

Because both splits occur from time to time, our diagram has to look like the following figure.

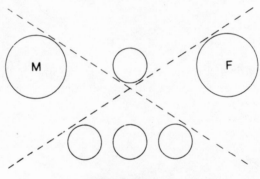

3½-6 Years

The thinking of children at this age is magical, that is to say, it is not reality-based, and they have trouble distinguishing among what actually are feelings, thoughts, and actions. Their thoughts, especially their angry thoughts, scare them. Nightmares are common. Children worry that others, like their parents, know what they are thinking and that they will retaliate. This magical fear of retaliation causes the child to worry excessively about body integrity and body damage. Any cut or scratch is a disaster. This is why this age is often called the "bandaid" stage.

During these frustrating fours and fives, most children and their parents do have a lot of fun. The child is animated, uninhibited, and imaginative, and enjoys interacting and playing. On the other hand, the child can cause stress between parents and among siblings and have trouble sleeping, having nightmares or wanting to sleep with parents. One minute you love and cuddle the child, the next you feel like giving him or her away to the nearest stranger. All of this is normal.

By about age six, most children begin to find preliminary answers to the question "Who am I?" Little girls begin to learn that they are to become "just like mommy" and enjoy playing this role. They give up wanting daddy all to themselves and look forward to some day having someone just like their father. Little boys begin to learn that they are to become "just like daddy." They give up wanting mommy all to themselves and settle for the idea of having someone just like their mother some day. Although some of these self-assessments may later change, it is through this process of identification that children learn to become more or less like the parent of the same sex. (The child in a single-parent family may have more difficulty working through this stage of development. Most make it through, but if you think that consulting a mental health professional would help, don't hesitate to get advice yourself and, perhaps, help for your child.)

During this time most children are struggling to establish basic assumptions about their identities. Parents also now do their imprinting of stereotypical sex-role behavior. If a boy reaches for a doll to play with, he is brusquely told that boys play with trucks or guns, not with dolls. Cultural clichés like this always amaze me—adult men must know how to relate lovingly to their children, among other people, not how to use guns, and adult men know that. Adult women must know how to express themselves productively, not just how to use eye-makeup, and adult women know that. Still, little girls learn that they play with dolls and do things in the kitchen; they do not work with tools or excel in sports. Girls also learn that it is acceptable to express love and sadness, but not self-assertion or anger; boys learn just the opposite.

Fortunately, the consciousness-raising efforts of the women's liberation movement have helped to free more and more families from the need to pass along these stereotypes. Children must feel free to explore and to learn many roles in becoming fully developed males or females. They must learn that true maleness and femaleness has nothing to do with the things one does or how one expresses different emotions, but with the kinds of resources and experiences one has, the kinds of relationships one can sustain, and the respect one develops toward oneself and others.

Toward the end of this stage, at about age six, two changes take place that help the child master the process of individuation. The central nervous system takes a large maturational leap forward, and this helps the child to move from nonreality-based thinking to reality-based thinking. Contradictory feelings and thoughts can no longer coexist with equal power. The child begins to understand that feeling or thinking one thing means that he or she cannot believe in its opposite at the same time and with equal conviction. In other words, the realization dawns that one cannot do or be two (or more) things at the same time. The child can now distinguish between reality and fantasy. One may pretend to be Superman, but one knows it is only pretend.

The other change involves the child's emerging awareness of the various accumulated value judgments that he or she has learned. At about this age, these fuse into an established conscience, called the "superego." This "voice," or conscience, stays with one throughout one's life, and becomes increasingly significant. It "tells" the child which thoughts, feelings, and actions are acceptable and which are not. Initially, the parents teach these values, and the child usually adopts them fairly automatically. He or she may rebel, but that is more because the child wants to do what he or she wants to do, not because any serious questions about moral or intellectual validity come up. In adolescence, as we shall see, these values are routinely reviewed and reconsidered.

Latency

Once the child has mastered the third task of development, individuation, he or she moves into a period of consolidation. Sometime around age six, the child becomes free to move out of the family and into the community. With the major psychological work of childhood done, the child's energy is freed to range more widely, in school and other learning activities, and in expanding relationships. This period, which lasts about six to eight years, is the *latency* period, illustrated in Figure 8.

During the latency period, children learn to relate to adults other than their parents and to children other than their siblings. They begin to focus on relationships with children of the same sex, and may ignore or move away from peer activities that include children of the opposite sex. Boys prefer boys and often don't like girls.

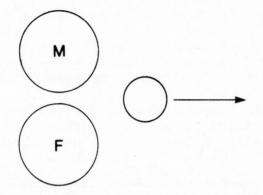

Girls prefer girls and may avoid boys. Very intimate "chum" relationships develop, and the child's behavior that you got used to during the individuation stage changes completely. A boy will shrug and push mother away if she wants to cuddle him; a girl may feel uncomfortable if father tries to hold or kiss her. Two boys or two girls may walk down the street arm in arm as "best friends." During this period children explore and learn the ability to relate to people of the same sex and form both intimate and casual friendships with them.

By the age of twelve or fourteen, this period of consolidation ends. Adolescence arrives, and with it, new tasks to master. Everything is about to change—possibly for the worse, but eventually for the better.

Normal Adolescent Development

Adolescence is a difficult time for almost anyone going through it, and for almost all parents. The period of adolescence prepares a person to move out of his or her childhood and into adulthood, and this transition has to be unique for each generation. Parents often rely on their own models and experiences, responding to their teenage children as their parents did to them or as they think they should have been responded to. The difficulty is that these role-models and experiences more or less successfully prepared today's parents for the last third of the twentieth century. Today's adolescents have to learn to live in the twenty-first century. You will have to speculate right along with your teenage children on the strengths, attitudes, and skills that *they* will need for *their* adulthood. Your own experiences will be out-of-date and probably too restrictive.

As parents of adolescents, you must teach your youth the values that you believe important, but you must also take into account the unique issues your teenager struggles with in the world as it is now and as it will be.

The adolescent must rework most of the psychosocial tasks of childhood. Physical growth still plays a major role in the stages of psychological growth. Some adolescents go through these stages with little or no difficulty; others have problems with a stage, then regroup and move forward.

Problems with Physical Change

It is useful to distinguish between puberty, the period of physical changes, and adolescence, the period of psychosocial changes. Ideally, the two occur hand-in-hand with each other. However, with some teenagers, these processes get way out of sync. When one is out of phase with the other, the person has to cope with even more stress than usual.

Think of the girl who at ten or eleven is taller than all of the other girls, full-breasted, and already menstruating, or the seventeen-year-old boy who is 5 feet 5 inches tall, with peach fuzz and a high voice. Both are physically normal, but each is at a different end of the normal growth curve. And each has additional stresses to cope with. The reverse is equally bad. The boy in sixth grade who is already almost six feet tall and growing a beard, or the short, flat-chested young woman who still looks like "a little girl" as she graduates from high school—each must cope with more than their share of the stress that adolescence normally brings.

Just as children do, adolescents have feelings and thoughts that cause conflicts and tension, but their physical growth has also given them capacities for action and reaction that no child has. When a six-year-old boy cuddles with his mother, he feels pleasant sensations; when a fourteen- or fifteen-year-old boy does so, he may be embarrassed when he has an erection. A little girl can thoroughly enjoy sitting on her father's lap, but a thirteen-year-old girl who does so may have physical sensations that worry her. Wrestling with or tickling a sibling of the opposite sex can become both sexually stimulating and distressing. These new reactions that come with physical maturation may be so upsetting that the adolescent feels forced to transfer the relationships that cause these feelings to "safer" people outside of the family.

The same is true for angry feelings. It is one thing for a little boy to feel rage at his mother when his eyes are at the level of her knee caps. It is another situation when the angry adolescent realizes that he is taller and bigger than his mother and that he can really hurt her.

The distress and loss of confidence caused by these physical and emotional changes encourages the early adolescent to become more dependent on home and parents. But the same newly discovered emotional feelings and physical reactions make it more difficult to explore and work out relationships and problems with parents and siblings. Thus there is conflict—within the child, and eventually within the family.

Initially, the early adolescent may attempt to cope with all this by using fantasy, choosing to relate to people who are unavailable and therefore safe. Boys and girls have "mad crushes" on movie stars, rock musicians, and sports heroes. The probability of a rock-music star suddenly knocking on the door of an adolescent girl and asking her for a date is remote enough to allow her to safely fantasize a relationship with him. Gradually, however, the young adolescent will begin to explore relationships with real, potentially available people. At first these interactions are likely to occur within groups, then within smaller groups, and finally with individual people. Very early dating is usually narcistically motivated: the adolescent wants to date someone who makes him or her look good—the cheerleader, the football hero, someone whom everyone thinks is desirable. Often a boy behaves toward his date much as he would toward boy friends, clowning around, showing off, or hitting them. Later on, both adolescent girls and boys will date someone who makes them *feel* good. Looks are still important, but less important than personality.

Independence

The first task of adolescence is to move from being a *dependent* person to being an *independent* person. The initial struggles often revolve around the established concepts of sex roles and identification. The old techniques that the child used to master separation may turn up again.

Negativism reappears. "No, I can do it myself." "Don't tell me how long my hair can be." "Don't tell me how short my skirt can be." This negativism is a renewed attempt to tell first you and then the world that this growing person has a mind of his or her own. And again it becomes an active verbal way of expressing anger. Adolescents seize on almost any issue to show that they have a mind separate from that of their parents. Parents and adolescents may argue about choice of friends and peer groups, school plans and courses, points of philosophy and etiquette. Clothing and hair styles have always been favorite issues with which to prove one's independence. The casual or unisex theme of today resembles the "cause" of every other generation—the "flappers," the "zoot-suiters," the "rockers," the "hippies," and so on. Each generation recalls how they used clothes, hairstyles, and other external badges, the more shocking the better, to show their parents they had minds of their own.

All the old struggles over expressing love and anger reappear as new issues. What do you have to do to be loved? To keep love? To show love? What do you do with angry feelings? All of these questions have to be worked through with family and friends. In the process, the adolescent begins to develop more consistent concepts of relationships and styles of expressing feelings. The adult personality is beginning to emerge.

In the process of gaining independence, the adolescent probably needs to reject the parents' values and to reformulate her or his own value system. Unless this happens, the adolescent's parents remain with him or her forever in the form of the conscience programmed in as a child. Teenagers need to rework these previously accepted values to fit with their todays and tomorrows. They will probably reject their former values at first, pointing out contradictions in their parents' values. They may feel that "no one over thirty can be trusted." They may challenge their parents for giving conflicting messages. "What do you mean, all people are created equal—you get mad at me if I date someone who's Jewish [or Protestant or Catholic, black or white or Hispanic or Oriental]." Or "Why should I be honest—you cheat on your income tax." Or "Why shouldn't I drink—you do."

This interim "vacuum," when old values are rejected and new ones have not been established, can be upsetting. Some adolescents temporarily take refuge in "prepackaged" systems: "born-again" Christianity, Buddhism, pacifism, the Boy Scout oath and laws, or some other value system or ritual. For others, their peer group provides this interim system. Closed "cliques" often set rules about all kinds of behavior—how to dress, who to talk to, who is "in," and who is "out."

Slowly the adolescent begins to blend many different values from all kinds of sources into his or her own existing values. By young adulthood, a new conscience, or superego, is established. The compatibility and flexibility of this new superego strengthens one's ability to handle and express feelings and emotions in relationships. All through life one's superego will have to be able to change and grow in order to accommodate new life situations.

As the adolescent begins to feel independent of his or her family, and as the family supports and encourages this emerging maturity, the question of the three-to-six-year-old is heard once again: "Who am I?" The answer, of course, can no longer be "just like mommy [or daddy]."

Identity

Thus the second developmental task of adolescence, establishing one's *identity*, begins. Becoming a "chip off the old block" isn't enough. Unlike the child, the older adolescent will select characteristics from many people—religious leaders, teachers, neighbors, relatives, parents, friends, maybe even famous people—blending certain of their features with her or his own to become a unique new person. This new person, or identity, is not one's final self, but it forms the basis of what one will become. One's identity must be reworked throughout life as roles change—one must adjust to becoming a graduate, a spouse, a worker, a parent, a grandparent, a retiree—and as experience buffets one about.

Each generation and each culture exerts different social and cultural pressures on human beings. The child growing up in the Victorian era heard very different messages from the outside world than did one growing up in the "wild" decade of the post-World-War Twenties. The adolescent growing up in the post-Vietnam world of the Eighties experiences different social and cultural standards than her or his parents did. Let me note once again that it is crucial for parents to understand and accept that their adolescent lives in a different world than they did as adolescents.

The total developmental process that began at birth culminates in an identity for each person. If your child successfully masters all of these tasks, he or she will have a successful functional identity with healthy and positive feelings about himself or herself. If any tasks are not successfully mastered, this identity can be restricted or dysfunctional.

Intimacy

The adolescent has one remaining task to master. Until this time, relationships have been based primarily on a child-adult model. Now the adolescent or young adult has to learn how to relate successfully to other people, and eventually to one other person, as equals, on a one-to-one basis. This kind of relationship is often referred to as *intimacy*. The task starts in late adolescence, but it is not complete until young adulthood.

When people relate in a dependent-independent mode, they need and depend on significant and more powerful people, like parents. When you are young, you may very well feel as if you and your parents are one. This is intimacy, but not a workable kind of intimacy in an adult world. In an adult intimate relationship in the independent-independent mode, each person depends on the other. However, even though each loves, leans on, and needs the other for his or her emotional well-being, neither loses his or her boundaries. At all times, each can still function independently and well. This is a goal that most of us work on all our lives and few of us achieve with total success. But because it represents the best that human beings can make of their adult relationships, it makes a fitting close for our discussion of normal development.

6

Psychosocial Problems for the Child with Learning Disabilities

The child who has learning disabilities has more than school and classroom problems—he or she has total life disabilities. The same problems that interfere with reading, writing, and arithmetic also interfere with emotional and social development or can cause emotional and social problems. Some infants may be halted in the earliest stages of development. Some children a little older may hesitate, unable to move forward through subsequent stages. Still others may develop within normal expectations, showing adequate progress at first, then be set back by a situational stress, like that of entering school.

Problems in Early Stages of Development

Infancy may be very difficult for the child who will have learning disabilities—remember, although irritability or Hyperactivity may show up early, the learning disabilities have yet to be discovered and are still "invisible." In Chapter 4 we looked at a number of problems of early infancy that result when the nervous system remains immature. We also saw some of the damaging effects these problems can have on the earliest parent-child interactions. (One mother's experiences are described later.) Babies with motor problems will be more floppy and poorly coordinated. Poorly coordinated infants may also have difficulty sucking and eating. Infants who are also Hyperactive thrash about, their constant activity creating constant problems with care.

We do not know what the full impact of perceptual disabilities may be during the early months of life. It is possible that an infant's auditory or visual perceptual problems interfere with its ability to learn about his or her environment. This, in turn, can delay the links to the parents and the establishment of *basic trust*.

Mastering separation requires at least two things: First, the child must feel secure enough to venture out and explore the world; second, this world must be attractive enough to make the child want to stay out there and engage with it. The child with perceptual and/or motor disabilities and possibly Hyperactivity cannot build the confidence to explore a world which must seem far too difficult to enjoy. If such a child has difficulty with either or both experiences, *separation* will be delayed.

Learning disabilities, along with possible Hyperactivity, Distractibility, or symptoms of an immature nervous system can cause stress to develop between parent and infant. Under these conditions, the baby is unlikely to be successful in establishing basic trust. When this happens, it cannot develop the confidence or feel secure enough to move away from its parents. To compound the problem, because the baby is having these difficulties, the parents are tempted to overprotect it, fearing that it cannot make it on its own. Sometimes the parties at both ends of the umbilical cord won't let go.

Then what happens when the child does venture out? If one cannot do what other two- or three-year-olds can do, or cannot understand what people are saying, or cannot communicate clearly or express oneself, the outside world will seem like a bad place to be. It certainly will not be experienced as positive or fun. Who can blame a child for retreating back into the safety of the home?

The result may be a child who prefers to stay at home. When things don't work out in nursery school, the child resists going, or, if forced to go, avoids the other children or interacts poorly with them. As these children struggle to master separation, you may see the negativism, the power struggles, the need to control, and the difficulties with relationships that were normal for age two persisting into ages three, four, and beyond.

What about the next stage, *individuation*? If the child is having difficulty with other children, with play activities, and with preschool situations, the steps in development that are normal for individuation will start late and may last long after the appropriate age. Other children will have long since outstripped the child in their emotional maturity. Even after age six, he or she may continue to be fearful or to try to divide adults and other children—problems that normally occur between ages three and six. When these immature behaviors still take place in kindergarten or in the first and second grades, teachers quite understandably become angry, and classmates too tend to fight with the child.

If no one has yet spotted their disabilities, boys may have a special problem with becoming "just like daddy." (The problem may be a little less pointed for girls.) The son who does poorly in games and sports may become irritable and prefer staying home with mother. Father is disappointed and lets his son know it verbally or nonverbally. The son senses the message and feels that he cannot be what father wants. If this happens, he may not be able to complete the individuation stage successfully, or he may do so, but with less confidence in himself than he needs.

Some children master each stage of development more slowly than most, but they may still have problems. They enter the *latency period*, and grade school, with some weaknesses in their psychological foundation, so to speak. Each new task causes stress, which, in turn, causes a temporary retreat to earlier behaviors. The child with problems may not consistently lag behind. A break in development or a retreat to an earlier behavior can happen at any stage along the way, even up into adolescence. Some children will have so much difficulty reaching these landmarks in psychosocial growth that professional help will be needed.

Emotional Problems

I find it helpful in understanding children with learning disabilities to realize that they have had only one brain all their lives, and they don't know that it is different from anybody else's. People yell at them, telling them to sit still, to pay attention, to keep quiet, to speak up, but they can't understand that they are more active, or distractible, or hard to comprehend than any other child is. They try just as hard to learn. Why don't they succeed? Their experiences confuse and frustrate them. Why do they constantly fail? Why are they constantly embarrassed? Is it any wonder that they develop emotional and social difficulties?

The special-education team points out that Billy has visual perceptual or visual motor problems. These learning disabilities interfere with his mastery of reading and written language skills, they say. We are used to focusing on problems such as this. But what about Billy on the playground who misses the ball because his eyes can't tell his hands what to do? How do the other kids react to Billy's clumsiness and poor performance? How does Billy feel when he is the last one to be chosen when the kids pick sides?

So it is with Allison. Educational and language evaluations identified her auditory perceptual and expressive language problems, and based on this information, the school has developed a specific educational and language therapy program for her. But is that enough? What happens to Allison when she is with her friends? She misunderstands what they say and responds wrong. Her friends think she is not paying attention or is dumb, and they exclude her from their games. Furthermore, although someone explained her auditory and language difficulties to her teacher, no one ever told her parents. So they too get angry with her for "not paying attention." What does this do to Allison? How does this shape her friends' reactions to her? How must she feel in the family? What does she then think about herself?

All too often such problems are not correctly diagnosed. Even more often they are not communicated to the right people in the right way. The child goes on experiencing repeated frustrations and failures. Finally, he or she develops emotional problems and is referred to a psychiatrist or other mental health professional for an evaluation. It is essential to distinguish between a child whose emotional problems are *causing* school and academic difficulties and a child whose emotional problems are the *consequence* of these difficulties. When learning disabilities are present, we are usually dealing with the latter case. But, of course, for some children the emotional and social problems which started as consequences of unrecognized and untreated learning disabilities eventually take on a life of their own.

As you read about the kinds of emotional problems children with learning disabilities can develop, think of your daughter or son. If you recognize any of these symptoms or behaviors and you have not already asked for help, discuss the situation with your family doctor or a mental health professional.

Withdrawal

Some children deal with frustrating life experiences simply by trying to avoid stress. The child uses a withdrawal reaction to avoid any potentially frustrating or uncertain situation by drawing back from it and becoming passive. He or she becomes unavailable for learning.

Because of her unrecognized learning disabilities, although she had a superior intelligence eight-year-old Bobbie had failed several times and was currently starting second grade. When I asked her what she did in school when she couldn't do her work, she replied, "When I was younger I used to crumble up my paper and cry. . . . Then they teased me and called me a crybaby . . . so I decided that school was no fun. . . . Since I couldn't leave I sat and pretended that I was home in my room with my dolls. . . . I made up stories and had a good time." The teacher complained that this girl would "daydream the day away if I let her."

Regression

Other children avoid stress by retreating to an earlier stage of psychological or social development. Earlier behaviors or immature, infantile interactions—things you think the child has completely outgrown—recur. The parents of seven-and-a-half-year-old Debbie complained that their daughter had been happy and normal until she entered kindergarten. As the mother explained it, at this point "she had a change in personality. She had trouble keeping up with her work. In first grade she just didn't learn much so now she's repeating first." The father added, "Home life is terrible. We yell at her all the time. Since school began this year, she's gone backwards, acting like a baby, talking like a baby . . . it's impossible. . . . She won't listen and tunes me out. . . . She's begun to wet her bed for the first time since she was three. . . . She even eats with her fingers." At a therapy session, Debbie talked about school. "I have trouble because I don't understand the work, especially reading and the math. . . . It's hard and I can't do it. . . . The teacher yells at me all the time. . . . Maybe I'm just not as smart as the other kids."

Displacement and Projection

Children may try to avoid the stress, the conflicts, and the feelings of frustration and worthlessness by displacing the reason for this failure onto something else. Some develop fear reactions. Their over-all, school-related feelings seem to take on specific meaning. Rather than experiencing a general anxiety or depression whenever she or he is in school, the child develops a localized fear that can be named. Eddie, for example, became afraid of a particular child on the school bus who always teased him. Once this fear crystallized, he could make sense out of the feelings he had when he woke up to go to school. When this happens, the child feels no better, but at least he or she does not have to endure the nameless fears and general anxiety that go with his or her unexplained and upsetting school failures.

Some children focus their anxiety on bodily functions. A child may develop stomach aches, lower abdominal cramps, headaches, diarrhea, or frequency of urination or bowel movements. These complaints often occur only in the morning of a school day, never on weekends, holidays, or during the summer. These children have to leave class to go to the school nurse or to go home. As with any physical symptoms, the discomfort is real. The pain goes away when the child is allowed to stay home, not because she or he was faking, but because the stress has been relieved. Katie, who was around seven at the time, once explained, "Sometimes I get into trouble because I forget to do what the teacher said or I erase too much. . . . The teacher yells at me and I get scared. . . . Then my stomach starts to hurt and I have to go to the nurse." Franklin woke up each school day with severe stomach cramps and vomiting. His mother kept him home from school and the pains usually disappeared by noon. A complete medical work-up found Franklin perfectly normal. He must have guessed why he was brought to see me. His first words were, "I know my stomach trouble is because I'm afraid of school. . . . Only it really does hurt . . . no kidding!"

Other children may explain their anxiety by focusing on their increasing awareness that something is wrong with their bodies. They have heard parents, teachers, and doctors talking about their brains or their nervous systems, and they have been through countless examinations and tests. So they express their hypochondria as complaints about body difficulties: "My back hurts," or "My head aches," "My knee feels funny." Sometimes this concern with their bodies extends into a general concern with body image or body damage. At times these complaints become a complete rationalization for failure: "I can't help it if I made a mistake—my arms hurt today."

But I didn't hear you . . . I was thirsty

Children might also avoid stress by becoming paranoid and projecting their feelings and thoughts to others. Teachers, class-mates, books, desks, all get blamed; everyone is out to get them or show them up. When Joe was ten and in a special class, he had frequent episodes of explosive behavior. He hit people, yelled, and threw things. His usual explanation was that someone was talking about him or making a face to try to get him into trouble. At home he refused to go out and play because the neighborhood children were always talking about him. A review of his school history revealed that two years earlier he had been a sad, withdrawn boy. One year ago he was described as an angry child who continually criticized himself. A psychiatric evaluation found that he was cer-tainly not psychotic. This was simply his latest in a series of at-tempts to cope with his problems by blaming others in a paranoid manner.

Children may also use their diagnosis as the excuse for their problems. They have heard everyone use various labels to describe certain of their behaviors, and they fix on these labels to explain everything about themselves. Such a child may explain, "I'm brain damaged so I can't do that."

The child may also generalize the disability into a sense of total worthlessness. "I'm just no good—I can't read." When confronted by a teacher with an error on a math paper, one girl responded, "I can't do that—I'm a retard." A twelve-year-old boy explained why he didn't have friends: "I'm brain damaged so I can't catch a ball too good. . . . All the kids play ball and since I can't play, I don't have any friends."

Weak Self-Image

Some children with learning disabilities do not develop a defense system competent enough to help them handle the pain of frus-trations and failures. As a result, they may experience a true sense of depression. Their failures, their inadequacies, and their poor interactions with peers and significant adults leave the child feeling angry and devalued. Younger children who are often unable to internalize anger may express their depression by irritability and aggressiveness toward everyone. Older children may exhibit classic symptoms of depression. They appear sad, cry easily, and may have trouble sleeping and eating. Sometimes the child turns so much anger inward that she or he becomes self-destructive or su-icidal. David, an eleven-year-old boy with learning disabilities and a long history of failures was referred for evaluation because of his overly polite, passive manner. During the evaluation he described himself as a "bad troublemaker . . . I'm stupid and I can't do anything right." This, of course, was in marked contrast to his usual overly serene behavior. He added, "I get so mad with myself when I make a mistake, I send myself to my room. . . . Sometimes I punish myself by making myself go to bed early or looking up my favorite TV show and not letting myself see it. . . . Once I got so mad I slapped myself."

In many children, their conscience, or superego, takes on a punitive tone and prevents them from accepting praise. If a teacher compliments a piece of work, the child feels compelled to destroy it.

When children keep these anxieties and feelings of worthlessness inside, they understandably develop a poor self-image. The child sees himself or herself as an inadequate, bad, worthless person who can't do anything right. Feedback from the outside world often encourages this self-image, and, at the very least, it does nothing to help correct it. One markedly depressed ten-year-old boy with such feelings had been Hyperactive since birth. Ronnie was always all over the place, his mother reported. "All he ever heard from me was 'no' or 'don't' or 'bad boy.' " Ronnie was kicked out of nursery school for being a "monster." He grew even wilder in kindergarten, and no better in first and second grade. Still undiagnosed, he repeated second grade, started third, and was then suspended from school. He had never known himself to be anything but bad, dislikable, inadequate, and stupid. The fact that he was very bright didn't change his self-image. No one can talk these children out of their self-assessments because the self-image results from a collection of real experiences. They can improve, however, when they begin to see the changes that come with appropriate help and when they begin to master learning and behavioral tasks.

Now twelve, Arthur had been diagnosed at five as having learning disabilities. He was placed on medication (we discuss psychostimulants in Chapter 12), and received several years of intensive special educational therapy as well as psychotherapy. When Arthur eventually went back to a regular sixth-grade class and did well, he reminisced, "Remember when I was at the special school and you kept telling me how smart I was? . . . I thought you just wanted to make me feel good because I couldn't read or do anything. . . . I almost gave up and I felt that I would just never make it. . . . Then one day something clicked and I started to read—I *really read.* . . . Then I started to do math. Boy, I could really learn just like you told me. I must have grown five years that first week I started to read."

Other Common Defense Mechanisms

When some children have difficulty dealing with anger, they may choose an indirect way of showing it. One such style we call "passive-aggressive." The child's behavior is not actively aggressive in and of itself, yet the child makes everybody angry with him or her much of the time. Dawdling and always being late is one good example of this. While supposedly getting dressed, for instance, the child may play with his or her clothes until a parent becomes furious. The child then looks up in bewilderment and says, "Why are you so mad at me? I didn't do anything." A special-education teacher once said to me of such a child, "He was so cooperative and helpful and sweet that I felt like bashing him in the teeth."

Other children become "passive-dependent." Initially the child avoids failure and unpleasant feelings by staying out of the situations that could result in failure. But this passivity can expand into a veritable life-style. He or she avoids taking any initiative in anything and minimizes getting involved in everything. A truly helpless child arouses sympathy in adults. The passive-dependent child's behavior often makes people angry because the helplessness appears to be deliberate and contrived.

Another common approach some children use to handle stress is "clowning." Clowning serves several functions. It can be a way of controlling feelings of inadequacy—the child clowns around to cover up feelings of worthlessness and depression. By playing the clown or freak, the child seems to be saying, "They call me a clown or a freak, but that's only because I choose to be one. I really can turn it off if I want to, but it's too much fun this way." If the child succeeds in this behavior, he or she disrupts the lesson or is told to leave the group, thus avoiding the academic work, and therefore the failure, that may have produced the stress in the first place. Frequently this wins a certain measure of peer acceptance. Suddenly the child everyone teases is the class hero. Thus the clowning is reinforced.

In some schools, the reward for being sent to the principal's office is well worth the effort—no school work, talking with the secretary, delivering messages, or playing with the typewriter. After four years of special educational and psychiatric help, Jack returned

"I can't"

to public school and was doing well. He returned to visit me, and I asked him to describe what he remembered about his previous school problems. At one point he said, "Boy, were those teachers stupid. Anytime it was my turn to read or do anything I had trouble with, I would tease another boy or joke around. It worked great. I got sent out of the room." Then he added, "Only you got me to see that I was the stupid one. . . . You can't get help if you're not in class, and I sure didn't want to spend the rest of my life in a special school."

Children with learning disabilities who are Hyperactive and/or Distractable are likely to develop an impulse disorder. The normal child learns with age to delay longer and longer between the initial impulse to act and the actual behavior, gradually building on past experiences to choose an appropriate behavior. Hyperactive children, however, tend to remain explosive or aggressive and to have temper tantrums. Some may be emotionally fragile, shouting or crying at the slightest frustration. Sometimes the child with this disorder breaks things or hurts someone unintentionally, simply because he or she moved or acted too quickly without thinking.

These impulse-disorder children may show other signs of their problem: stealing, bedwetting, fire-setting, hoarding food, or excessive eating. An eight-year-old boy who was Hyperactive continually broke things and had one tantrum after another. Mike had all of the other symptoms too: bedwetting, hiding food at home, stealing money from his mother's pocketbook, and setting fires. When asked about the fire-setting, he reflected his own concern with impulsivity and impulse control when he explained that what he enjoyed most about it was "letting the fire get big and almost ready to burn everything up. . . . Then I would put it out before it exploded all over the place."

Occasionally such children appear to act overly mature. Faced with feelings of being different and inadequate, and fearful that because of this no one will take care of them, these children decide to grow up quickly. Often they have a compelling need to be in control and become upset if they can't control every situation. They look, act, and relate to others like serious little adults, and this behavior may pay off: Adults compliment them and spend more time with them. His parents described one seven-year-old boy as not needing anyone to take care of him. Chuck was totally independent—in fact, he took care of everyone else in his family and his school class. He enjoyed most having discussions with his teacher. He had no sense of humor and was described as "a perfect little man," completely self-sufficient. In a psychiatric diagnostic session, Chuck's fantasy and play reflected great concern about dependency needs and a fear that no one would meet them. So he *had* to take care of himself. Chuck had denied his anger and his wish to be taken care of and was using all of his emotional energies to maintain his protective facade.

Social Problems

All of the emotional problems we have been looking at profoundly affect a child's social relationships. A few other special types of social problem also deserve mention here.

Often children with learning disabilities prefer to play with younger children. Because they cannot handle the interactions or participate in the activities of their own age group, they intuitively seek out an age group whose skills they can manage. A boy of nine might have visual perceptual, fine motor, and visual motor disabilities, but good strengths in auditory perception, language, and gross motor areas. He goes out with his classmates but finds that he cannot play baseball or basketball well enough to keep up. Then he learns that five- and six-year-olds do a lot of calling to each other and prefer running, climbing, and riding bikes. These gross motor activities and interactions he can handle. In addition, the younger children look up to him, while his peers avoid or tease him.

Another special social problem relates to the child's difficulty in reading social cues. These children don't seem to pick up the subtle, and not so subtle, signals—facial expressions, body postures, tones of voice—that suggest that they need to react differently or to change their behavior. Joking around goes too far, feelings get hurt, and tempers may flare. These children miss the cues that nonverbally say "Enough!"

We do not yet understand the reasons for this problem with reading social cues. Whatever the cause, the lack of such an ability creates major difficulties for a child who must learn to make his or her way through the world more skillfully.

In Closing

The pain that children can experience because of their frustrations and failures is real. Unattended to, it can have a major impact on personality development. Without help, these feelings and thoughts can shape behavior both for the present and the future. Let me illustrate with another case example.

Bob's parents were concerned. He was eight and had just completed second grade. He had done poorly in first grade, not learning to read or to print well. During second grade he made some progress in reading but was not yet up to grade level.

"He seems intelligent," his mother reported. "But, Bob's so angry and unhappy. He's a perfectionist and gets upset if he can't do his school work." The consultation with me followed a conference requested by the principal. She spoke of Bob's high anxiety level in school and of his poor self-image. The principal thought that he had an emotional problem and that he needed psychotherapy.

His father told me that Bob set very high standards for himself. "If he can not do things he says he is no good or stupid. Now, he's so afraid that he won't do well that he avoids trying any new activities."

When I went out to the waiting room to greet Bob he stood up and shook hands. He was a very serious and tense child who behaved more like an adult than an eight-year-old. As we entered my office I tried to help him relax by encouraging him to choose a toy or game to play with and by chatting with him about general things. He went through the motions of setting up some toys but preferred to sit on the floor with me and talk.

The following is an excerpt from a tape recording of this session. To make it flow smoother, Bob's statements are noted; mine are in parentheses. Throughout this session he was verbal and serious and showed signs of being tense (twisting his fingers, frowning).

(Tell me about school.) I don't like to make mistakes. (Oh.) I get angry and frustrated. (What do you do?) Sometimes I feel like crying but I tough it out. (You can't cry?) The kids would think I was a baby. (What else do you feel?) I get angry with myself. I say I'm dumb or stupid or can't learn. (How do you feel when you say these things?) Bad. I'm just a jerk. (What do you do with these feelings?) I distract myself until they go away.

(Bob, why do you think you feel this way?) I don't know. (Could it have something to do with school?) I don't read or do math too good. (And the other kids . . . ?) They do it easier. (When you say that you look upset.) Yea.

(What else happens in school?) I get scared sometimes that the teacher will be angry with me. (I see.) If she doesn't like my work she sends me back to do it again. I get mad because I did my best. (What do you do?) I distract myself and push it out of my mind. Then I do the work. (How do you push away such angry feelings?) I get busy with the work. (Don't you feel like yelling or throwing something, or . . . ?) No, that would be bad.

(You know, Bob, I get the feeling that you don't like yourself too much.) There's nothing to like. (You mean you cannot think of anything about yourself that is good?) I guess I'm alive. (As I listen to you I begin to feel very sad. I wonder if you feel the same way.) Yea.

(How do your Mommy and Daddy feel?) They love me. (Oh?) I'm their child. (And that's the reason.) I guess. (You guess?) Well, sometimes I think that Mommy wanted a girl because they don't cause as much trouble as boys. But, they may want a boy to carry on the family name. (So, you may not like yourself and now I hear you say that maybe your parents don't like you either.) Sometimes I think that.

(You know, Bob, I think the real problem is that you don't like yourself.) Yea. (And, you look so sad right now. How long have you had such feelings and thoughts?) I think they started in first grade. (Tell me about it.) I couldn't do some of the work. The teacher use to make me do it again. The other kids got smiles from the teacher. I just got disappointed looks.

(What do you think was the problem in first grade?) I don't know. (You seemed to have trouble doing the school work.) Yea. (You know, Bob, I've worked with other boys and girls with problems like yours. Sometimes they worry that their problems are because they are bad and being punished or because there's something wrong with their head or maybe because they're dumb or retarded. I wonder what kind of thoughts you have.) I do think about these things. (You look so sad when you think about these things.) Maybe. Sometimes I think that maybe I'm retarded. (Retarded?) Yea. (That would be pretty upsetting to think that you were retarded.) Yea. (Maybe we had better find out what the problems are so that you won't have to worry about things that may not be true.) I'm just too dumb to learn anything. (I can see why you might think that way. Only, I bet you can learn. Only, maybe something is getting in the way. I'd like to find out what it is so that we can do something about it.) I can't do anything right.

Last year at the pool I hit my head a couple of times. . . . (And, maybe that caused the problems?) Maybe that's why I'm so dumb. (I don't think that's the reason you're having trouble in school. But, then, I guess it's hard for you to believe me.) There's no hope for me.

At this point in the session I put Bob in my lap and held him. He finally began to cry. I reassured him that I would help him and his parents to solve his problems in school so that he could like himself again. I told him that I thought he was a pretty nice kid and that it hurt me to see him in such pain.

Formal testing identified Bob's visual perception, sequencing, visual memory, and fine motor disabilities. There was scatter on the IQ test. He was of high average to superior intellectual potential. Special educational interventions were developed for third grade; his teacher would be briefed.

But the damage to Bob's self image and psychological development had already been done. He was sad, hurting, and in need of help. Psychotherapy was begun, but not for the reasons given by his principal—he was not primarily emotionally disturbed and therefore having trouble in school. He was learning disabled, and his trouble in school caused him to be emotionally disturbed.

This therapy, however, would not be successful without the special-education interventions in school. How could I help him rethink his self-image and feelings about himself if he continued to have failing experiences in school?

7

Psychosocial Problems for
the Adolescent
with Learning Disabilities

If your son's or daughter's learning disabilities were first recognized in childhood and he or she got the help that was necessary, you are ahead of the game. Adolescence is a stressful time, but it is less so if the basic educational, social, and family supports are in place and you can build on them. If your child's difficulties were not recognized until a major behavior problem surfaced in junior high school or high school, your task is going to be much more difficult. With the adolescent's problems compounded by late diagnosis and by the physical changes of puberty itself, it is even more critical to move in with a full team evaluation and a comprehensive program.

During adolescence, the fact that a learning disability is a total life disability takes on even greater meaning. It affects every kind of life involvement and interaction. Adolescents whose problems were recognized and treated during childhood must now handle new challenges. Those youngsters whose problems went unrecognized until adolescence have a double problem—they must deal with their existing disabilities while trying to compensate for the academic and emotional price they have already paid.

The adolescent with learning disabilities has special problems.

Early adolescence is characterized by a strong need *not* to be different. The person who, as a child, cooperated peacefully with a special-education routine may, as an adolescent, suddenly refuse to continue to take part in any special programs and insist on being in regular classes. He or she may refuse to take medication. You may have to come up with some creative compromises: switching special tutoring or other remedial help to an out-of-school, and therefore less public, setting, or allowing the youngster to administer his or her own medication rather than going to the school nurse.

Adolescence is a time of rebellion, and it is certainly an especially painful period for an adolescent with learning disabilities. As parents, you will often be in no-win situations. If you insist that your child act his or her age, the adolescent suddenly acts like a five-year-old. If you baby her or him, the adolescent suddenly erupts in anger. If you try to help, the adolescent wants to be left alone. If you leave your child alone, the adolescent accuses you of not caring. My best advice is to accept the fact that you can't win. Talk over this whole matter frankly with your adolescent and try to struggle through together. If the rebelliousness gets quite out of hand, you can fall back on professional help.

Developmental Stages

In the Western world at least, emotional stress is to be expected during adolescence. The adolescent with learning disabilities has even more emotional problems than the normal adolescent. I have already emphasized the importance of distinguishing between emotional problems which *cause* academic problems and those which *result from* academic problems. The learning disabilities have earlier resulted in frustration, failure, and behavior problems. Now the behavior problems that resulted may have taken on a life of their own, growing to such proportions that they have made the adolescent unavailable for learning. Both kinds of problem must now be resolved.

In addition, left-over problems from infancy or childhood may resurface. We have talked about the normal developmental tasks of adolescence, moving from dependency to independence, and establishing one's identity. Adolescents with learning disabilities are more likely than most to have trouble in all of these areas.

Independence

Becoming independent—or separating—means going out from the family and realizing successes and positive experiences on one's own. An adolescent who is insecure, who has a poor self-image, who does poorly with his or her peers, may not be able to move away from his or her family comfortably. Instead, some adolescents simply embrace their dependency, turning away from outside companions, into the home, and putting on an appearance of being contented—even preferring—to be alone or to watch television. Others find these excessive dependency feelings upsetting and fight them, internally, or by lashing out at others. Negativism, power struggles with adults, and unacceptable clothing, hairstyles, and choice of friends are often ways of expressing one's fear of and discomfort with dependence. Although you may find all of this behavior quite irritating, don't turn off completely. It is extremely important that you understand and try to help.

As you try to help your adolescent through this struggle for independence, keep in mind his or her specific strengths and weaknesses. For the youngster to find out that one can and must succeed on one's own, you must work together to maximize successes and growth-producing experiences. You may have to rethink chores. And you will want to work with the adolescent in selecting after-school activities, sports, or jobs very carefully.

Learning disabled adolescents face special problems with their friends. If they too understand what they can and cannot do well and feel comfortable in talking with you about these things, you can help them to map out special strategies which will help them to succeed on their own.

For example, Cathy, who was now fifteen, wouldn't go out with her friends to get a snack after school or out to a restaurant on the weekend because she couldn't read the menu. We discussed this problem in family sessions. Cathy's sister suggested that she pretend she didn't know what she wanted and wait until last to order. This would enable her to listen to the others order and pick from among their choices. Her father suggested that he could copy the menu from the local fast-food places so that she could practice reading it at home. She tried both approaches right away, and they both proved helpful. Later, as she became more comfortable with her friends, she shared her problem with a girl to whom she felt particularly close. This friend understood and began to help too. When the gang was at a restaurant, her friend would turn to Cathy and say, "Gee, I can't decide if I want a pizza or a meatball sub or spaghetti. What do you think"

You probably never stop to think how many situations call for quick facility in reading, but they are everywhere: one must be able to read street signs or maps, for instance, or bus stop signs, TV listings, or movie marquees. If your child has a reading problem, it is essential that you all come up with imaginative suggestions for handling it.

Understanding and acting on spoken instructions is another skill that everyone must have to get along in daily life. If you can't comprehend what you are told, your opportunities for action and for learning shrink to almost nothing. Here again, if your adolescent has this problem, some creative solutions are in order.

Seventeen-year-old Rico had auditory perception and auditory short-term memory problems. He went for his driver's license test. He knew how to drive, drove well, and passed his written test with ease. There he sat behind the wheel waiting for the road test. His father got out of the car, the examiner got in, sat down beside him, and said, "OK son, listen to me. See that white line? Pull out, then bring the car to a complete stop at the white line, then turn left and go to the stop sign. Now, do it." Rico misunderstood some of the directions and couldn't remember the rest. He failed the test.

Rico's father suggested that he speak to the examiner and tell him about his learning disabilities. He thought that perhaps the examiner would give Rico written instructions instead of oral ones. Rico, however, refused to be treated differently. That night he and his father worked out a compromise. They went back to the test site, talked with several people after they had completed the test, and learned the routine. Rico's father wrote it out, step by step, and Rico memorized it. He reapplied for an appointment, and when he took the test the next time, he passed with ease.

Whether the task is using public transportation, learning to shop, cooking, handling money or a check book, driving a car, or interacting with friends in everyday activities, work with your adolescent to develop strategies for coping with the tasks he finds difficult. Building on strengths and compensating for weaknesses is critical because a sense of self-confidence, self-image, and finally, a sense of independence are all based on these small and large successes. No one can write an instruction booklet for *your* adolescent and *your* family. In fact, no one really can tell your son or daughter how to do things best—the disabilities to be overcome are theirs, as are the tasks to be accomplished. But you can help in every way possible as they write their own books.

Identity

Once some sense of independence has been achieved, the great task of adolescence is that of finding an identity. This is difficult at best in a world where value-systems change, career opportunities change, and options expand and diminish unpredictably. The adolescent of today—as of any day, for that matter—questions some of the current "adult values," wonders what you have done to make the world the way it is, and shares in rather more than less uncertainty about the future.

Much of this is just like what you experienced when you were an adolescent. But in some ways the world that today's adolescents face is quite different from that which you encountered. Sexual values and the importance of relationships have changed. College no longer "guarantees" the opportunity for social and economic advancement. Family life in the future will probably be more mobile and family structure more flexible. In terms of jobs, productivity may be much harder to identify with a person's individual effort and input.

Under these uncertain circumstances, what kind of identity can an adolescent establish if he or she feels like a failure at school, with friends, or within the family? Any learning disability only exacerbates the problem. Such adolescents can hardly be blamed if they remain immature and childlike in their behavior. They may be bland and passive, showing no personality, or they may be quite unstable, changing their minds constantly, not knowing what or who they want to be. But if they cannot be blamed, they cannot be excused. With the proper help in school and understanding, support, and help at home, these problems can be worked out. If not, professional help will be needed.

We have said that adolescence is a time when no one dares to be different. Being just like everyone else is a criterion that must be met before a sense of difference and a pride in individual differences can emerge. This emerging sense of identity as a person, of course, is a big step toward growing up. But learning disabled youngsters are already different, and their social problems are innumerable, especially where their peers are concerned. They have difficulty taking part in sports, in dancing, and most other activities that their peers are involved in. They often lack social skills. Making small talk, maintaining eye contact, listening to others, waiting for someone to finish talking before they speak—all of these abilities are critical to social acceptance, and the adolescent may have mastered none of them. They may misunderstand what is said, make inappropriate remarks, or forget what a conversation is about. They may be bossy, aggressive, and belligerent, or so quiet and passive that they fade away in any group.

None of these behaviors leads to easy peer acceptance, and instead of pushing in the right directions, some adolescents withdraw into the house, content with TV, listening to the stereo, or reading. Others will be so desperate for social acceptance that they may act inappropriately and get into trouble: Girls may become sexually active in an effort to get attention and "love"; boys may try acting "tough," hanging out on the fringes of a gang or getting involved in petty crime.

None of these problems are easy to solve. Fortunately, most children cope with adolescence well enough to make it. Some, however, remain misfits until—and even after—they become adults. Usually things improve about this time, however. The stress of school may be past history. The pressures and demands on adults are different, and the nonathlete or the quiet person may be more valued, or valued for different qualities.

As parents, the best you can do is first, understand that your child is going through his or her first identity crisis. If you try to understand the problem, it may lead to an understanding of the behavior. Help your daughter or son seek out activities, sports, and other programs that offer her or him the best chances of success. Keep communication open, and set up some systematic ways that you can work on solving problems together.

Many adolescents, in fact, will find techniques that they can use to help themselves. For one thing, they have to accept the fact that they have to work harder than other people to do even simple things, and they have to bring themselves around to an attitude that makes this work seem like fun. Some of their techniques for coping may seem compulsive—keeping things neat, well-organized, and perhaps overly planned, for example.

I cannot think of a better example than Ron. He had just about every type of visual perceptual, organizational, sequencing, gross, and fine motor problem possible. He had been in a self-contained special-education program since early grade-school. Now, in tenth grade, he started in a small private regular high school. We worked together during this year. Ron was determined to make it. He negotiated with each teacher to get the adjustments he needed. He worked three to four hours each night to accomplish work that most of his classmates did in two. Every assignment was carefully organized. If he had a report to do, he would block out specific time, often weeks earlier, for library work, reading time, outlining time, writing and rewriting time. For lengthy reports he dictated to his mother who then typed the material.

Ron was making it. He was bright and got good grades. Toward the end of the year his English teacher asked each student to write an "autobiography" that could be given to the eleventh-grade English teacher as an introduction. But let Ron tell his own story. Note his self-confidence and learned ability to problem solve, compensate, and cope.

I look at Ron and I see a young man with a great deal of will power. One can see this in my drive to overcome the limitations that impede my learning. This is also seen in my capabilities and successes. I am what is frequently referred to as learning disabled.

The first thing one sees about me are my many limitations. One of my learning limitations is that I cannot spell. Although I have tried for many years to learn through memorization, key words, phonetics and other teaching devices, I cannot spell. I remember taking a spelling achievement test year after year and staying at the same grade level.

The next limitation I have is that I cannot write legibly, even to myself. For instance, I remember taking a biology test, putting down what I knew were the right answers, and getting the paper back marked 10 of 25 and "can't read." Another limitation that affects my schoolwork is that I cannot calculate quickly or write quickly, even illegibly.

Some of my limitations have nothing to do with school, but concern my athletic ability. I cannot hold a canoe paddle correctly and coordinate the movements of my arm so that the canoe does not go in circles. I cannot coordinate between the sight of the incoming ball with my eyes, the level of the bat and the swing of my arm. Consequently, nine times out of ten, I miss the ball completely. This problem manifests itself on the other side of the batter's box as well. I can keep my eye on the ball, follow the ball, see the ball come to me, put out my glove and miss the ball from three to nine feet.

I try to overcome my limitations through coping with them. With spelling, as previously described, I cannot learn how to spell. Even using a dictionary is hard for me because I cannot figure out the first two letters of a word. I find that the best way to cope with this problem is to inform teachers of it and whenever possible, have someone who knows how to spell around. As for handwriting, although I have tried to produce a form of legible script, under the careful and patient tutoring of many, I found that this is next to impossible and my writing looks like a cross between chicken scratch and arabic. Therefore, whenever possible, I type my papers, thus eliminating the necessity for legible handwriting. To cope with my problem in calculating, I use a calculator, thus eliminating any careless arithmetic errors or C.a.e.'s as they are called. I remember going to my math teacher after class one day and saying, "I can do this work; I understand the concepts, but I just cannot physically do the computations."

As for my athletic coordination, I try the best I can. I remember being out on the lake one day, alone in a canoe. A brisk wind arose and I was trying to go from one side of the lake to the other in a perpendicular line to this wind. This situation was made doubly frustrating because I knew I should point the canoe upwind of where I wanted to go, but could not manage to keep it pointed in that direction. I try to cope with my problems playing baseball by going out to the field when no one is there, tossing the ball as high as I can and trying to catch it.

Despite my limitations, I have many capabilities and have had several successes. I have an ability to grasp the general concepts which a teacher is trying to explain. I have been able to write essays and papers that are clear and concise. I can learn from my mistakes and from constructive criticism of my work. And, if genuinely interested in a subject, I will try to find the most information I can about it. I also have a good memory and retain factual information. I am highly motivated to get things done not only on time, but early, if possible, and am equally highly motivated to learn.

My successes are many. These include my school work, where I usually get either A's or B's, of which I am very proud, and fighting my own battles with teachers to make them understand my limitations. I have some sports related successes, also. These include my sailing ability, which enabled me to pass the sailing requirement for a patch at a summer camp I attended. At the same camp, I learned to become a fair shot and passed the four lowest shooting levels in a relatively short time. And if I couldn't paddle a canoe, I developed an ability to row, a simpler and more enjoyable form of human powered water activity.

My most recent success at school includes surviving, if just barely, a rather confusing three days with a science teacher, thanks to the help of an English teacher, and surviving by not going crazy at the thought of what I cannot do.

Recognition of my capabilities has led to an urge to overcome my limitations and has produced many successes. I admit, however, that I could not have succeeded without the encouragement of many people.

Let me amplify Ron's next-to-last paragraph, the one about surviving. His science class went on a one-week trip to a nature program. Each day the staff lectured on different topics. Ron wanted to learn, but he could not write as fast as the speaker spoke. Soon he was lost and couldn't understand the demonstrations or the assigned projects—for example, "Now go out into the woods and look for examples of the symbiotic relationship I just discussed." He asked his biology teacher for help. She sent him to the instructor. The instructor seemed puzzled and didn't know what Ron wanted. By the third day Ron was so frustrated that he stormed out of the class muttering to himself about the stupid teacher. He walked off into the woods, angry at himself for being so unable to handle the situation. Why hadn't he explained his needs to the instructor? What would he do if he didn't learn everything? How would he ever make it in college with all that lecturing? All his old doubts and fears resurfaced. After a time he decided he needed help. He went to his English teacher, someone he felt close to and trusted, and explained his problem. His teacher went with him to the instructor and discussed the problem. The English teacher agreed to take notes for Ron who was then freed up to listen. The rest of the week went well.

As you watch your adolescent grow up, talk to other parents whose children have similar problems, to your family doctor, to the special educators at your school. If you have more trouble than you can manage, don't hesitate to seek professional mental-health guidance.

Hyperactivity and Distractibility in Adolescence

Hyperactivity and/or Distractibility appear to improve or disappear in about 80 to 85 percent of children at puberty. We do not understand why. In about 15 to 20 percent of the cases, however, these conditions continue through adolescence and possibly into young adulthood.

If this happens to your son or daughter, he or she will probably continue to need medication. You may face resistance—as we said, nobody at this age wants to be different. You can usually handle such a problem by talking it through with your teenager. You might try allowing some time off from the medication as an experiment. That way you can see just how important the medication is, and your son or daughter can see for himself or herself, too.

You might come up with a plan for using medication in a more targeted way. Figure out those four-hour time periods during which Hyperactivity and Distractibility are most likely to interfere with normal activities—either in learning or in social situations. Your adolescent then might agree to use the medication during those targeted times but try going without it during other times.

If the medication is really needed almost all of the time and if your child still resists, discuss the problems with your physician and get counseling.

Learning Disabilities in Adolescence

If learning disabilities have gone unrecognized and untreated, the adolescent is likely to develop psychological difficulties. Some adolescents may lie about and avoid homework or get into acting-out problems, cutting classes or getting in trouble with the authorities. Some of these young people who need special help, sadly, get the message that the school doesn't want them and they quit. I call them "school pushouts" rather than school dropouts. The school so neglects and abuses them that they give up and leave. Once out from under the pressures of school, they may settle down, get a job, and somehow conquer their behavior problems on their own. In the best of all possible situations, they take a high-school equivalency test later. But, unfortunately, without professional help, most will continue to have difficulties.

As you know, learning disabilities affect more than school performance, they affect all aspects of one's life. What help, then, should the schools provide and what can be done in the home?

Many learning disabilities do not go away as your child gets older. When they persist, special help must also continue. For some, self-contained or special placement programs are still necessary. For others, regular classes with supportive special education therapy will be enough. Some students need books recorded on tapes, people to take notes for them in class, or more time to do assignments or to take tests. Each student has different needs. Be sure that your school provides what is necessary and that you and your adolescent understand the program he or she is in.

Let me add just one aside. Unfortunately, many school systems invest their time and money in programs for elementary school children, offering minimal help for the high-school student with special needs. You must work on this. Become an advocate for the programs that your child needs. If your child needs them, doubtless others do too. Even if you can afford the private help necessary to supplement the deficiencies in your high-school program, don't be content just to do this. Get together with other parents and try to develop an appropriate program *within* the school.

If your adolescent's problems were not diagnosed until high school, he or she probably has major gaps or holes in basic knowledge which have to be addressed. If your child did not learn that $2+2=4$ early in elementary school, she or he won't be able to understand that $2a+2b=4c$ in high school. The same is true for basic grammar and punctuation rules.

You and the school will have to assess the future realistically. Where is your son or daughter? Where can you expect him or her to be by age eighteen? Should you encourage college, a technical school, or vocational training? Discuss this with the school professional staff or a private consultant, and make sure that your son or daughter participates in the decision and the planning. If your youngster is moving toward a trade or a job, ask the special educator to advise you on the strengths that different career choices require. Here, as elsewhere, everyone must build on strengths and minimize the impact of weaknesses.

If college is possible, you should know that many excellent two- and four-year colleges will accept students with learning disabilities. They base acceptance on the student's potential, not just his or her grades. (See the Appendix for a list of these.) These colleges offer special tutoring, liaison with the college teachers, and resources such as books on tape. You can arrange for the Scholastic Aptitude Test (SAT) to be taken on an untimed basis and/or with a preceptor who reads the questions and records the answers. (Information on requesting this is in the Appendix.) Competent, motivated people with learning disabilities can go as far with their educations as they wish to. It takes work—more work than the average student does—but it can be done. Programs and resources are available today for all levels of schooling, including graduate and professional schools.

It all boils down to this. As your son or daughter gets older, he or she must begin to accept some and later most of the responsibility for his or her own life and well-being. As self-image and identity emerge, that advocacy becomes inescapable. No one else is on the front line, and no one else knows better what he or she needs. You must help your adolescent learn to speak for herself or himself and to fight for what is necessary. You cannot do your adolescent's job for her or him any longer, and now is a good time to face this.

The Learning Disabled Adolescent as Advocate: John

At seventeen, John was a high school senior, in regular classes but taking two hours a week of private special-educational therapy. John had been in special programs since the fifth grade. He was a bright young man with disabilities in visual perception, sequencing, and fine motor areas. His oral reading ability was at about fourth-grade level.

When John began his senior English class, he met with his teacher and explained what he could and couldn't do. He requested permission to have more time when taking written tests in class. He explained that he would get his homework in on time because he would take the extra time at home. He did not, he said, want to turn in unfinished tests in class, however, and he volunteered to come in early or come back during lunch or after school to finish them. He asked to be trusted to not cheat or pass the questions on to others. He also asked that he not be called on to read out loud in class.

As the semester progressed, the teacher had the students reading literature assignments and writing reports on each one. John did this, and did it well. Each week, however, the students had to take turns reading their reports out loud in class. John was not excused. At first he memorized his reports. In class he pretended to be reading as he recited his material. As you can imagine, this soon became a major time drain, and it seemed counterproductive to John. So he stopped memorizing his written work and approached his teacher again to explain his wish to avoid reading in class. The teacher insisted that John read, and John firmly refused.

John worked hard and got an A on each report and on every exam. In spite of this, he received a B at the first marking period. At this point, he called me for advice, and we worked out a strategy. He asked if I would come with him when he went to implement our plan. I told him that I would role-play the situation with him and help him in any other way I could, but that it was time for him to fight his own battles. I assured him that he could do it.

John requested a conference with the teacher and the principal. He started the meeting by telling the principal that he had received a B in English. Then he asked the teacher what grades he had gotten on each report and test. The teacher acknowledged the A's. John opened a folder and showed the principal these reports and exams. Then he asked the teacher why he received a B rather than an A as an over-all grade. The teacher replied that the grade was also based on class participation. When John asked for clarification, the teacher replied that John had refused to read his reports in class.

Calmly—we had rehearsed this before—John asked the teacher if he was aware that John had learning disabilities and, specifically, a reading disability. The teacher said that he knew of this but thought that if John wanted to be in a regular class, he had to be like all the other students. John took a deep breath and said, "I wish to advise you that if you do not change the B to an A I will file a legal suit against you for discriminating against the handicapped based on Section 504 of the Rehabilitation Act of 1973."

That night John called to brag. He got his A. He was pleased with his grade, and with himself. I was delighted with the confidence he had gained and the growth that his behavior reflected. Yes, his parents could have done it, maybe better, certainly in a more indirect style. But John needed the experience, and he got it.

8

---

*Family Reactions to
the Learning Disabled Child*

We have spoken at some length about the problems that learning disabled children and adolescents have in their relationships with people both outside and inside the home. The emotional and social problems of family members who not only want to, but have to deal productively with their afflicted daughters, sons, brothers, sisters, deserve special attention. As in earlier sections, I shall start here with the normal reactions of parents and siblings, then go on to look at the larger problems that arise when perfectly normal feelings linger too long or become too extreme, thereby becoming abnormal and destructive.

When one member of a family suffers, everyone in the family feels the pain of the sufferer and reacts to it, sometimes with nearly equal distress. Parents, brothers, sisters, grandparents—all are part of this human system within which the learning disabled child lives and grows. Everyone in the family needs to understand the full range of problems the child or adolescent has if anyone is to be of help. Everyone needs to understand her or his *own* reactions as well, and sometimes that is a painful and difficult process.

After your child or adolescent has been through an evaluation, someone on the evaluating team should explain the findings to you. The child, too, should know and understand, to the degree possible, what the findings are. Sometimes the evaluator takes care of this routinely. Rarely, however, does anyone, including the parents, explain the findings to sisters, brothers, and other family members. Yet it is imperative that everyone connected with the child know about and understand the problems.

As parents, you undoubtedly had difficulty accepting that your child was different, that something was wrong. You may have experienced, or may yet experience, a series of reactions not too different from the grief reaction that people have when someone dear to them dies, although this grief is of lesser intensity. In a way, this reaction is very valid. You must "give up" a part of your child, or at least your ambitions for the child that you fear may never be realized. As we talk about these reactions here, don't become distressed. These feelings are not only normal, they are to be expected.

We shall go on to look at many of the problems that increase the stress the family already feels over the basic situation. If you recognize that any of these are serious problems in your family, you would do well to consult with your family physician or a mental health professional. Above all, don't feel ashamed to discuss feelings that may seem "selfish" or "unworthy" to you. These problems are real and your feelings are genuine. You must look at them squarely and deal with them. Keeping a stiff upper lip, or denying that they exist, only makes things worse for you and for your family.

Normal Parent Reactions

It should not surprise you that in addition to being mothers and fathers, parents are also human beings. They have their own feelings and thoughts. They usually have mates with whom they enjoy intimate relationships, relationships which are often hard enough to manage successfully without additional stresses. Having a child with a disability stirs up feelings and thoughts, fears and hopes that most people are unprepared for. These reactions affect both the parents as individual people and as a couple.

At no point is the stress greater than when the diagnosis is made: this is the moment when parents feel the first rush of anguish, fear, helplessness, anger, guilt, shame—all at once. Nothing can describe the thoughts going through a parent's head as he or she rides home from the doctor's office after that first conference. No sensitive professional should ever describe a child's problems to a parent without acknowledging these feelings and ending with a positive course of action such as "and this is what we will do about it."

Unfortunately, not all professionals are this sensitive. Some play what I call the "Ha, Ha, you have leprosy" game. They throw out a lot of labels, banging a parent over the head with "Your child is retarded," or "Your child is disabled—goodbye." Out the parents go, overwhelmed, with little hope or direction to take.

Denial

The initial phase of the grief-like reaction to the discovery of a learning disability, as with other grief reactions, is often *denial*. "It can't be true . . . the doctor must be mistaken." Or, "She only saw him for an hour, I don't believe it." You may doubt the competence of the bearer of such news and want to punish him or her. Frequently parents seek other opinions. Although getting other evaluations is useful, unfortunately "doctor shopping" for someone who will tell you what you want to hear does not do anything productive for your child.

Another form of denial is the "cover-up" reaction. One parent, usually the mother, wants to "protect" the other parent by not sharing the results of the studies or by minimizing the problems. Some parents successfully cover up the fact that the child is in a special school program for years. Sadly, the mother or father who is uninformed about the child's true abilities often continues to build up unrealistic expectations and demands results of the child that the child cannot possibly produce. The child, seeing through this cover-up, perceives the true reason for it: "They can't accept me as I am; they have to pretend that I'm different than I really am." This often makes children quite understandably angry or sad, and they usually have difficulty accepting themselves when they do not feel that their parents can accept them.

Anger

A period of anger commonly follows the denial stage. Parents may direct this anger inward, against themselves, or project it outward, blaming the other parent or any other outside source. On learning of a child's disability, it is normal to feel anger and other sentiments such as "Why me?" "How could God do this to me?" "How could I have done this?" "How could *you* have done this?" "We never should have had children!" This initial reaction often reflects feelings of disappointment, helplessness, and frustration which are quite real. Realistically, however, these feelings must and will pass.

Guilt

If parents have turned their initial anger inward, attacking themselves, turning anger against the self rather than against the problems, feelings of depression will probably follow. Associated with this reaction is a feeling of guilt. It is a very short step from "How could I have done this?" to "It's all my fault." The parent may berate herself or himself with "God is punishing me because . . ." or "I didn't follow my doctor's advice," or "I've been given this extra burden to prove my worthiness."

With some people, feeling guilty and/or depressed represents an attempt to establish control over a situation that they perceive as basically hopeless and out of control. If a parent can lay the blame—or attribute the cause—to him- or herself, that person then "conquers" the situation by explaining it, however erroneously. The "logic" is that if this happened for a reason—on account of something one did—and if one does not practice that transgression again, then nothing like what has happened will happen again.

Just as the child who feels depressed tends to become quiet and to pull away from people, so the depressed parent becomes isolated. If this depression is allowed to continue, the parent may withdraw from the child or the other parent at just the time when one or the other, as well as the other members of the family, need that person the most.

If initial anger has been displaced outward, the parent enters into a pattern of blaming or attributing the fault to someone or something outside herself or himself. Like the guilt reaction, blaming an outside agent at least places responsibility *somewhere*, and this too protects one from feelings of helplessness. The parent may blame the physician because "He didn't get to the hospital fast enough," or "I told her I was in labor, but she wouldn't believe me and I almost delivered in the car," or "If the pediatrician had come out to see him rather than prescribing over the phone he wouldn't have had that high fever." A person may generalize this reaction to all professionals, who then became "bunglers," "incompetents," and "charlatans." "It's the school's fault," or "She's just a young, inexperienced teacher," or "He's just a rigid old fool." The teacher or doctor or whoever is the butt of anger probably never hears these complaints. But the parent may never allow *the child* to forget them. Reactions such as these undermine the child's faith in and respect for the very people he or she must turn to for help and for hope.

Some parents attempt to suppress their guilt or their need to place blame somewhere else by overprotecting the child. The most normal, human thing to do when a youngster is hurting is to reach out and try to protect her or him. This is necessary and helpful. But one's goal must be to protect the child only where she or he needs protecting and to encourage the child to grow where he or she does not need protecting, even though that may be painful. A blanket of overprotection covers the child's weaknesses, but it also smothers the child's strengths. Not only does overprotectiveness keep a child immature and delay growth in areas where that is possible, it also makes a child feel inadequate. He or she knows what's happening. When everyone else has a chore to do but your daughter does not, when eveyone takes turns clearing the table but your son never has to, that child will very probably conclude, "See, they agree with me—I *am* inadequate." Such children may be poorly coordinated or unable to concentrate for any length of time, but they are as sensitive as you are, and maybe more so.

Most parents do work through these normal denial, anger, and guilt phases. When they do, they gradually become strong advocates for their children, mobilizing their energy in constructive ways.

Pathological Parent Reactions

Chronic Denial

Some parents cannot give up their denial. They continue to "doctor shop" in a continuing search for the doctor with the magic cure or for someone who will say that nothing is wrong with their child. Such parents greet the newest professional on the block with flattery and praise, criticizing the many doctors, educators, psychologists, and psychiatrists whose opinions they have rejected. Ultimately, the new savior too is rejected and then attacked. As their frustration grows, they hop from one promised cure to another, often becoming the victims of those who capitalize on people in distress. This hopeless "shopping," of course, deprives the child of time that should be spent in constructive programs and the valuable therapy that he or she needs.

The chronic denial reaction has other potentially serious consequences. Because each "authority" fails, she or he must be downgraded when the parents move on to the next one. The child picks up the message not to have faith in anybody in any professional capacity. This faith and trust is absolutely necessary in order to have hope, and hope is absolutely necessary if one is to work toward overcoming the handicap. And, as I said before, the child also picks up that subtle but clear message: "We can't accept you as you are. . . . We must find someone who will tell us that you are not the way you are." The child hears, knows, and reacts with anger, shame, and a conviction of inadequacy.

Chronic Guilt

When a parent handles his or her unresolved guilt by becoming overly dedicated to the child, that parent is apt to be covertly furious about it. What comes across in public is the dedication: "No task, no trip, no expense is too great to help my child." What comes across behind the scenes is the anger at having to do all this, and at having to give up things. Occasionally, a parent becomes a professional martyr: he or she never lets anyone forget how great the effort, how selfless the sacrifice. The surface behavior may be sweet and admirable, but somehow the child picks up the bitter parallel message: "Look how much I do for you, you ungrateful, good-for-nothing child. You're worthless to begin with, and you show no appreciation."

Chronic Anger

When the parents don't resolve their initial anger and learn to handle it, they continue to project it. Nothing can go right. Someone is always wrong in their minds: "After all this time and money, you haven't helped my child? How come?" Or, to the child: "After all my efforts, why can't you learn anything?" Such parents, miserable themselves, are almost impossible for professionals to work with—or for a child to live with.

For other parents, the normal initial reaction of overprotecting the child might become a life-style for the parent, one which both prevents growth for the child *and* the parent and increases the child's feelings of worthlessness. Under these circumstances, the child can easily become infantilized. Occasionally overprotective behavior may stem from a parent's attempt to cover up feelings of his or her own inadequacy as a person and a parent. People with low self-esteem and feelings of worthlessness may achieve feelings of being wanted and needed by deluding themselves that they are "all the child has in the world." When the child's existing immaturity and feelings of incompetence lead to failure, he or she naturally retreats back into the home. The overprotecting parent sees this and feels even more justified in moving in and protecting some more. A self-defeating cycle begins to repeat itself, the child increasingly realizing that she or he is helpless without the parent, and the parent reinforcing the notion that the child cannot survive without him or her.

In a closely related behavior, a parent may handle unresolved guilt by withdrawing from other social and/or family contacts and totally dedicating himself or herself to the child. Some parents carry this to the point where they have almost no energy left for relationships with the other children in the family or with their husbands or wives. Taking care of the one child's needs becomes so demanding and taxing that the person is too worn out, too weary, to meet the needs of the other children or for social or sexual relations with his or her spouse. The result is a dysfunctional family. And once again, often the anger at this state of affairs is not openly discussed between the parents but displaced onto the child who is seen as the cause of it all.

The Reactions of the Other Children in the Family

When parents suspect a learning disability and become concerned, they usually take the child to one or more specialists. Finally someone explains to them what the problem is and what needs to be done about it. At some point, someone probably sits down with the parents and "interprets" the findings. Occasionally, but not often enough, someone sits down with the child and explains to him or her what the problems are, what the events of treatment will be, and why. Almost never does anyone explain any of this to the child's brothers and sisters. Yet they are part of the family, and they need to know. As we know, when one member of a family hurts, everyone hurts. When they are left in the dark, what are brothers and sisters supposed to do? How might they react?

Some become very worried and feel *anxious*. This is especially true in families where the cover-up is on and little, if anything, is said. "What's wrong with Jimmie?" they ask, to which their parents say "Oh nothing special . . . it's OK." Yet they see the parents busing Jimmie from one place to another, and they hear them talking in hushed, worried, or angry tones. Occasionally they hear words like "brain damage" or "Where are we going to get the money for all of this?" They see mother or father upset, maybe in tears, maybe angry. Aware that something is wrong but not knowing what it is, their imaginations may take over. Frequently they fantasize worse things than those that are real. Then they worry. I have heard brothers and sisters say "Will he live? Is he going to die?" "Will it happen to me?" "If it's not important, why all the whispers and hush-hush?" Your other children must have clear information at a level they can understand, and all of the facts that they need in order to understand.

Sisters and brothers may become *angry*, fighting with the child who has the problems or with their parents. If double standards are in effect, you can be sure they will notice them and become angry. "How come I've got to fix my bed and she doesn't?" or "He broke my toy and you didn't do anything." Or the amount of time and energy that the parents spend with the disabled child may make the other child very jealous. Taking the one kid to special tutoring, special programs, and doctors, leaves little time available for the others. So much money may be spent on the handicapped child that everyone else has to do without, or vacations have to be compromised. One can't really blame the siblings for complaining.

Furthermore, these children will undoubtedly have to take some teasing at school. "Hey, how's your dummy brother?" or "Your sister sure acts funny . . . she's so gross . . . is she a mental case?" Anyone, and especially a child, is embarrassed by such comments and gets angry. Even at home, a normal sibling may not feel safe. Children may stop bringing their friends home for fear of being embarrassed by the antics of a brother or sister.

Sisters and brothers may feel *guilty*, too, and they may feel particularly guilty about their anger when the verbal or nonverbal message from their parents is "He can't help it," or "It's not her fault." This is a hard message to swallow for someone who has not yet gained a lot of perspective on life. Or a brother or sister may secretly think, "I'm glad it's not me," then feel guilt and shame for thinking such thoughts.

Because of these feelings of anger or guilt, a brother or sister might *act out* against their sibling with the disability. They may tease and provoke the child to encourage misbehavior, or they may do something themselves, then set up the child as a scapegoat. As the parents punish the handicapped child, the siblings feel revenged. Sometimes normal siblings set up the handicapped child to look or act bad simply because they think that the worse their sister or brother looks, the better they look.

A normal sibling can also affect the child with disabilities negatively. It seems to be the plight of handicapped children that a younger brother or sister is not only supernormal and delightful but precocious, quickly passing him academically and socially. That hurts. Yet, in all fairness to such children they must be encouraged to live up to their potential. They deserve encouragement and praise. Do not hold back or minimize praise for fear of hurting your son or daughter who has learning disabilities. They have to learn to cope with reality.

There is no way that you can prevent some or all of these feelings from surfacing in your family. None of your children were born self-denying, altruistic models of charity. Besides, all of these feelings, provided they are kept within limits, can be handled. The only way to forestall the worst of this anger among your children is first give them all of the facts, then let them know that it is safe and acceptable to express themselves fully about what they are thinking and feeling, and finally, answer their questions rationally and honestly.

None of this will be easy, but you are their parents too. If you see that you need help in explaining your situation at any point, don't hesitate to ask your family physician, special educator, or someone else to help.

An Example of Normal Family Reactions: Danny

I first saw Danny for an evaluation at age three, and I have followed him for the past ten years. Shortly after the initial evaluation, his mother began a diary. Initially she tried to reconstruct her experiences with Danny from the time of his birth. I have interwoven Danny's clinical picture with excerpts from that diary. Mrs. S. writes exceptionally well, often eloquently, but don't mistake this for a fictional account. As she confronts and finally begins to bring the various stages of her despair under control, you will be struck by the truth and validity of her account.

Pregnancy

Mrs. S.'s third pregnancy, after two sons, one four years old, the other two, went without complication. Her comments reflect the anticipation with which both parents greeted this child.

A 3rd son? What a joy, what a delight, such pride for the Father—what pleasure for the only woman—the queen in a household of adoring men. The other 2 are dark-haired and dark-eyed like Mom and Dad. The 3rd is a unique one with his blue eyes and strawberry blond hair. Grandma says he was meant to be a girl. Everyone agrees, "Well, if you had to have a 3rd son, at least he's different." We didn't realize at that time just how different he was.

Danny had the advantage of being the 3rd child. By the time a 3rd is born all of the anxieties implicit in the care and handling of a normal infant have vanished. No more fits of panic when the baby cries unexpectedly. Nor more wringing of hands at the first sign of a sniffle or loose bowel movement . . . just a placid, cool, nonchalant parent juggling baby on one arm, holding middle brother with right hand, pulling the wagon laden with sand box toys with the other, calling to the oldest son to look both ways while crossing the street on his bike. The combination of self-confident Mother and animated, stimulating surroundings are calculated to make this 3rd baby so happy, so comfortable, with none of the pressures or tensions that the other 2 had to endure. "They bring themselves up, these 3rd children do. He'll be your easiest," assured our pediatrician.

Delivery and the First Year of Life

Danny's delivery was normal, with no reported difficulties, and his physical examination prior to discharge from the hospital was also normal. Mrs. S. quickly noticed, however, that he was different from the other children—irritable, overactive, unable to focus. Feeding him was a problem, and often accompanied by his vomiting. The pediatrician treated him for colic. Danny also had trouble getting to sleep, and he often slept only three or four hours at a time. Sometimes he cried and thrashed about for thirty minutes to an hour. Holding him did nothing to comfort him. Several immature reflexes were present too (see Chapter 4). Danny's skin was overly sensitive to touch, and he had a tonic-neck reflex—

when his head was turned, the arm on the side he faced toward went up.

Mrs. S. reported that from the start Danny didn't like her. When she picked him up, he cried; the more she cuddled him the more he cried. When she turned his head toward her nipple, he pushed her away. She felt helpless, inadequate, angry, and guilty. She did not yet know about Danny's immature nervous system, nor did she understand his apparent hyperactivity and distractibility. So she blamed herself.

Well then, why did he cry so much? Why did he squirm in your arms as if pleading to be released to the security of his crib? Why the endless bouts of vomiting, before, after, during his meals? Why not the same show of pleasure at being rocked and played with like his brothers? Why no "coos" or "goos" or babbles or giggles? Where was this joyous, relaxed, happy 3rd baby syndrome?

By the end of Danny's first year of life I attempted to review all of these statements regarding the easy routine with 3rd baby—the enjoyment I was supposed to be savoring through him—the idea that "he's your last so lap it up" sort of notion. All I could come up with was a dull ache in the pit of my stomach. Why isn't he fun for me? Why doesn't he return my love? Why no give-and-take between baby and anyone? His constant crying and whining, his discontent and apparent discomfort, convinced me that he must be in some physical distress. That question, along with his persistent vomiting, brought me to the pediatrician who assured me that he was fine. I must relax and learn to loosen up. That along with a little sympathetic support was supposed to reassure me.

But the dull ache in head, heart, and stomach persisted. Why the relief for me at Danny's bedtime? Why the feeling of incompleteness when he was around and the feeling of solidarity and wholeness without him?

My growing conclusion was that there must be something wrong with me to result in this personality conflict. I was perplexed by my feelings of guilt in relation to this child, because if that were my pattern, why wasn't I feeling guilty in relation to my other children? I realized later that my guilt originated from ambivalent feelings toward him—feelings of love and hate, of sympathy and anger, of concern and fear. The insecurity that my relationship to him created inside of me resulted in feelings of self-doubt about my capacity as Mother and in regard to my own emotional stability which had never been in question.

My loneliness while submerged in these feelings was intense. In spite of a good marriage and a loving husband, I was alone. Many of these feelings and observations were not shared by my husband who wasn't with Danny as much as I—who never saw him vis-à-vis his age peers and who by virtue of a very placid, calm nature had a greater capacity to accept a wide diversity of behaviors. Every attempt I made to acquaint him with my concerns was met with assurance that Danny was fine—perhaps a little immature, but fine. The family reminded me that I was older when I had him— perhaps two kids had been enough, all of this being after the fact. All I was left with were doubts, fear and anger— directed toward myself and toward this creature who was the source of all my problems.

In looking back over Danny's first year of life, as well as those of others like him, it is difficult to pinpoint just what impact his learning disabilities had. Auditory perceptual disabilities were later diagnosed. What effect did they have on his orienting to sound or on his relating to or attaching to his mother? What effect did his auditory figure-ground disability have? Could Danny orient at all to his mother's voice? Mrs. S. describes her frustrations, confusions, and ambivalent feelings toward the developing relationship with her infant son. Could Danny's feelings have been any less troubled?

Year One and Two

Danny's language development was delayed. On top of everything else, he now became frustrated by his inability to communicate his needs. His gross motor development was also delayed, resulting in very slow mastery of sitting, standing, walking, and running. He remained Hyperactive and highly Distractible. He did not outgrow his hypersensitivity and became defensive, avoiding too much body contact. Possibly because of these neurological problems, he had trouble dealing with separation. Both parents found handling Danny overwhelmingly difficult. With no information and no reassurance from her pediatrician, Mrs. S. continued to search within herself for an explanation.

By 13 months of age a lock on his bedroom door was required to keep Danny protected from his own enormous fund of aimless energy which was consistently directed toward destructive pursuits. Perhaps his resentment at being locked in or an increasing hyperactivity was the cause of the extreme havoc he wreaked on his surroundings. Linoleum was lifted up off the floor of his room. Pictures in their frames were torn down from the walls, window shades were replaced because they were ripped up. A rocking chair was used to bang against the wall, thus creating dents in the plaster board. A harness held him down in his high chair and one was used in his stroller when he was reluctantly wheeled away from his exhausted Mother by an equally reluctant babysitter. And all the time I'm thinking what is wrong with me that I have created this child who I wish I never had.

The more I disliked him, the more he clung to me, the less able he was to let me go, thus causing horrendous scenes at my departures, serving to increase my guilt, and self-blame. "When I leave he gets so scared. Therefore, I shouldn't leave. But, if I don't I'll go mad. So I'll leave but he'll scream and I'll feel so awful." This internal dialogue characterized every separation we were ever to endure.

His constant aimless running resulted in many falls and bruises, the worst of which was a collision with Danny's nose and the dining room table. Sutures were required for that accident which was followed by several other close calls—all a result of his hyperactivity and poor coordination. Along with this went the assaults by Danny upon anyone who dared get physically close. Once he was seated on my lap I would in a 5 minute period of time receive several blows to my jaw from the unpredictable banging of his head. His frantic squirming discouraged me from holding him or cuddling him. Kicks on knees and in stomach, little hands pushing my face away from his—so many efforts to keep me away—all added up to one conclusion. He doesn't love me and I don't love him and it's my fault and it's unnatural and wrong and I wish I didn't have him and I've ruined my life forever. And yet, there he sat with his sad blue eyes and his confused forlornness. He was as unhappy as I was and I had to find out why.

Year Three

Danny's gross motor problems persisted. He began to develop language, but he often appeared to misunderstand or to respond in ways that made little sense. His parents felt that his thinking was more concrete than his brothers' had been at the same age. He developed fears of unknown places and of new objects. His separation problems persisted. Although toilet trained for bowel functioning by age two-and-a-half, he wet the bed at night (called "nocturnal enuresis"). He started nursery school.

At last Danny was 3. A new era was ushered in by his enrollment in a nursery school—relief for Mommie and some friends (please God, some playmates) for Danny. But more importantly, at last some objective feedback from emotionally uninvolved teachers who see normal 3-year-old kids all the time. No more would I have to rely upon Dad's calm assurances, upon Grandmother's accusations, upon my own frantic self-inquiry.

Several months passed before the teachers decided that it was time to confront me with reality. Danny was not involved with the other children, they reported. Furthermore he was tense, frightened, highly distractible and most of all, very unhappy. It was with mixed feelings that I received this news. On the one hand I was very upset to hear my worst suspicions confirmed. On the other hand I was relieved to hear that someone else saw the same thing—that my sanity and clear vision need not be held in doubt any longer. Most of all, I was grateful for the sense of purpose and motivation that this shared awareness endowed me with.

At this point the parents brought Danny in for consultation. In the course of the evaluation, his pediatrician and a pediatric neurologist, as well as a special-education specialist and a speech and language therapist saw him. I did the child psychiatric and family evaluations. The concluding diagnosis was Minimal Brain Dysfunction manifested by:

1. Specific learning disabilities (auditory, perception, sequencing, abstraction, auditory memory, gross motor, and demand language disabilities)

2. Hyperactivity, Distractibility, residual perseveration, and residual tactile defensiveness

3. Emotional problems (separation anxiety, fears, poor peer relationships)

4. Family problems (overwhelmed, frustrated, helpless parents)

The bedwetting at night was also noted. The team felt that this was possibly another reflection of his immature nervous system.

The following treatment plan was recommended, and implemented:

1. Special educational and language therapy in a nursery school for learning disabled children

2. A trial on a psychostimulant

3. Preventive family counseling focused on educating parents about their child's disabilities and about how to approach help

The medication, Ritalin, minimized the Hyperactivity and Distractibility. It also stopped the bedwetting. The parents learned to use deep touch stimulation when holding Danny, and this lessened his tactile defensiveness. He adapted to the new therapeutic nursery, and slowly his language improved. The long process of special-education therapy had begun.

Mrs. S. describes the evaluation and its impact. Her awareness of her feelings and the shift in her ways of handling them reflect the counseling.

It was these feelings that enabled me to have Danny evaluated. He was seen by many specialists, each seeming to focus on one part of his problem. By the end, all the parts came together and presto—a diagnosis—something to grab hold of—something to explain it all and most of all a means, a method, a way to help.

Danny's neurological impairment caused perceptual problems which resulted in learning difficulties, we were told. His restlessness, his dislike for being touched and touching, his chronic unhappiness and frustration all could be explained by this syndrome. The cause of it was unknown. So who could be blamed? There was a way to help him . . . please tell us how? There is a way to handle him at home that will make him feel good and happy and worthwhile . . . please tell me and I'll try. It will take time but he'll get better . . . or will he??? How great!

So, with all this, I gazed upon my neurologically impaired Danny, lifted my eyes to the heavens and whispered, "Thank you. It's not as serious as I thought. Thank you. There is help available. Thank you. He will in time get better. Thank you, again. You are not a crazy, unlovable, unnatural Mother. Thank you; thank you; thank you!"

But if that's the case, why didn't anyone believe or support me? Why was I kept in this state of anxiety and fear all these years? Where were the experts or even the loved ones? Why didn't they trust me? Why didn't they hear? And so once again I was angry—a state that was becoming second nature to me . . . descriptive of my mood and personality.

The anger directed itself inward then because it was futile and uneconomical to express it, I became sad, depressed, forlorn. In short, I felt pity for myself. Why did it have to happen to me? What did I do to deserve this? How will I ever find the strength to endure? How can I be a Mother to this poor, defenseless child? Days of brooding were to follow. I was caught up in a grief reaction that was all-consuming. I accused everyone of being unable to understand what I was going through. In a way I was trying to say, "Look how I am hurting. Won't someone take care of me and see how much I am caring?" The only problem with this behavior, I soon determined for myself, was that it accomplished nothing positive nor worthwhile and, furthermore, it led me to feel unattractive and selfish.

As soon as this awareness surfaced, a new era dawned. Self-indulgence, once completed, paved the way for the realization that Danny and I were going to be involved with one another for many years to come and that I'd better come to terms with his problem and begin to work on it with him so that both of us could be happier than we were. Thus, I allowed myself to become informed by the professionals, comprehending the "whys" and learning the "how-tos." With this knowledge came understanding and with this understanding came coping and with this coping came a growing sensitivity toward his positive changes and progress. This encouraged me to continue with renewed courage and with expectations for Danny, based on the reality of the situation.

No longer was there room in my rationale for unproductive self-pity, brooding, or accusations. I realized that the effects of this attitude would result in more problems. Let's then acknowledge that we have a problem. Let's not be afraid to label it, to explore it, to learn about it, to deal with it, and to accept it.

Years Three Through Twelve

Although Danny remained in special-education programs throughout the fifth grade, by the fourth grade he was in a regular educational program, receiving special-education and language therapy an hour a week. He remained on Ritalin. His parents worked closely with his school programs and his teachers over the years. They carefully selected those peer activities and sports that tended to build on his strengths rather than to magnify his weaknesses. Each year brought successes and new challenges. Mrs. S. reflected on these experiences:

But, does the acceptance defend a Mother against uncomfortable feelings? Does she ever adjust to the situation and simply continue her day to day existence, giving minimal thought or worry to this part of her life? The answer for this Mother is a resounding NO!

The process of adjustment is an ongoing one. On his bad days, I feel bad. Back creeps the old sense of fear and foreboding. On good days I feel hopeful and perhaps a trifle excited at the glimpse of health and wholeness I see under the surface. On most days I feel the responsibility of another day. I decided that I will try to begin at his beginnings—to love him to accept him right where he's at. I realize I must plan according to his needs at that moment and with this comes the task of ignoring some of my own. No one can do that without feeling some anger.

And what about the feeling of deprivation when you see how poorly he measures up to his age group, and, as he grows older, how poorly he stands in relation to children even younger than he? What of the feelings you get when you see him rejected by children and adults alike because he can't relate in the expected, conformist manner? What of the embarrassment you feel when his problems result in antisocial behavior in public? What kind of excuses do you force yourself to fabricate to ease your self-consciousness? What do you say to family when they assure you that all he needs is some discipline and he'll fall into line? The disruption he causes in the tempo of family life—the interference with certain pleasures arouses anger, deprivation, and guilt. And how about the emptiness in your gut when you catch a glimpse of his inner world of confusion and of loneliness? How does that make you feel?

With all of these feelings surfacing and resurfacing with every new situation how can one ever expect to be adjusted? The only answer I have found is to make room for the feelings, to accept them—not to luxuriate in them, but not to deny them . . . to say them out loud to yourself or to whoever is unafraid to hear them. This paves the way for a stronger, more positive relationship with Danny.

The way I relate to Danny becomes reflected in the way he sees himself. If I allow his problems to scare me, he too becomes scared. Communicating to him that he is worthwhile and lovable and that I have hopes for him enables him to face his future with hope and courage. This places a great responsibility on me, but it is the only chance any of us have for a good life. If we have hope for Danny, he will have hope for himself.

I still wish I had three perfect sons. I occasionally indulge in that "wouldn't it be lovely" fantasy. I have come to treasure in the other two what many people take for granted. I have a great investment in them but I do in Danny too. It is an investment imbued by the implicit faith I have encouraged myself to have in him and in me. It will take a long time and it will be difficult but I have hope that it will work.

Current Progress Note

When this book was written, Danny was in the eighth grade. Academically he was doing well. His peer relationships were limited and best handled one at at time. He related well to his parents and brothers but was described as "a little aloof" with others. He continued to need the medication, but his psychological functioning was at age-level.

Part Three

Diagnosis

9

The Evaluation Process

As I have said before, the child or adolescent we are discussing here has a group of problems often found together: learning disabilities, probably; Hyperactivity and/or Distractibility, possibly; and possibly other evidence of neurological problems as well. Most of these children also have emotional, social, and family problems due to their frustrations and failures at school, at home, and with peers.

To evaluate this person fully requires a team effort. This team may work in a medical setting, in a mental-health facility, or as a part of your educational system. Your physician might be part of this team or simply be the one who requests the evaluation. At times, the family physician coordinates a team evaluation by requesting different studies. If she or he initiated the study, your physician should synthesize the completed reports and review them with you.

Frequently, the school becomes concerned and initiates an evaluation. Ideally, the school special-education team contacts the parents, the family physician, and anyone else who has worked with your child. Be forewarned that you may have to push assertively for the necessary studies, then work hard to be sure that each person involved, the family doctor, the school, the mental-health person, communicate with each other. One hopes that all these people will interact. If they do not, however, you have no choice but to insist that they come together to form a working team.

I hope we have passed the point where children who do not learn well enough are routinely kept back in school. Repeating a grade may be appropriate for some children, but it should not be implemented until enough studies have been done to understand why a child is not learning. A child with a learning disability who is kept back, but who gets no additional help, may do no better the second time. Do not let the authorities at your school force your child to repeat a grade unless they have done an evaluation, unless they know why he or she did do poorly, and unless they have specific rationale for such an action. Even then, the school should consider moving the child on, but with special help, rather than keeping her or him back.

Now let us consider where to go to get an evaluation, who should be involved in it, and what you should expect from it. I shall also suggest ways to prepare your child or adolescent for such an evaluation. In the next chapter we go into more detail about the kinds of studies done by each evaluator.

The Evaluation Process

An evaluation should have three parts: the planning; the testing, observing, and interviewing; and the interpretation of the findings. First, of course, the parents should know who will see their child and why. The child must also know why he or she is being evaluated and, in general, what will happen. When the planning phase begins, the team members should together decide what questions need to be asked and who should try to answer them. For example, why is this child not mastering reading? Or why is she so distractable? Or why does he get into so much trouble in school? In order to do this adequately, the evaluating team must know as much as possible about just what problems the child is having.

During the evaluating phase, several different people see your child or adolescent to conduct formal studies. One person may observe him or her in school and/or get information from the classroom teachers. Someone else will meet with the parents to inquire into past medical, developmental, and psychosocial information and to explore the current problems. Other specialists, whom I itemize in just a moment, also test and observe the child. Finally, the information and impressions that result from these multiple studies must be synthesized. One person may share these conclusions and recommendations in an interpretive session with the parents, or the different specialists may summarize their findings. (Later I describe the way I prefer to conduct this interpretive process.)

Several professionals are involved in the team evaluation. A *special educator* trained in the field of learning disabilities evaluates your child to determine if learning disabilities exist and, if so, what types. This person also explores learning strengths and approaches for intervention in problem areas. These studies determine your child's performance level in certain skill areas like reading or math. If the special-education studies suggest difficulties in the auditory-language areas, a *speech and language therapist* (or *pathologist*) may do additional studies to clarify the difficulties and to explore possible treatment approaches. If the special educator's studies suggest that the difficulties are in the gross or fine motor areas, an *occupational therapist* may do further studies in order to suggest remedial treatment.

A psychologist tests and otherwise studies the child to clarify several issues. Does the child or adolescent show evidence of any emotional problem? If so, what is it? What is his or her level of intellectual functioning? What are her or his approaches to organizing, thinking, and problem-solving (often referred to as "cognitive style")? Often, the results of these tests do not provide a true reading of your child's abilities. Learning disabilities interfere with certain test performances, and they may lower certain scores. Once the psychologist takes this into account, however, the test results tell the level at which the child is currently functioning and what his or her potential can be.

Sometimes a neuropsychologist is asked to participate in an evaluation. This work might be done in place of parts of the educational studies. Like testing for learning disabilities, neuropsychological studies attempt to identify and analyze brain function. The results focus on the areas of the brain that appear to be functional or dysfunctional, and also note specific areas of learning strength and disability.

A *physician* should do a complete physical examination. In some instances a *developmental* (or *pediatric*) *neurologist* may examine the child or adolescent. A brain-wave test, the electroencephalogram, or "EEG," may be in order, although this is usually not done unless some suggestion of a seizure problem exists. If a hearing problem is suspected, an *audiologist* or a physician specializing in ear, nose, and throat disorders, an *ENT specialist*, may be called. If a visual problem is suspected in the areas of vision or muscle balance, for example, an *optometrist* or a physician specializing in eye diseases, an *ophthalmologist*, may participate.

The mental-health professional who sees the child might be a social worker, a psychologist, a psychiatric nurse, a generally trained psychiatrist, or a child psychiatrist. This specialist assesses the child's level of psychological and social functioning and explores any emotional conflicts or stresses with the child. This may or may not be the same mental-health professional who meets with the parents or the whole family to explore past history and current concerns.

Ideally, the full team then meets to discuss their findings, to establish a clinical impression or diagnosis, and to develop a treatment plan. One or more members of this team should finally meet with the parents and later, probably, the child too.

As parents, you must be sure that you understand all of the findings, and you must be comfortable with the recommendations. At a minimum you should have clear answers to the following questions:

1.   Does my child have learning disabilities? If yes,
     What are his or her learning disabilities?
     What are his or her learning strengths?
     How far behind is he or she in what areas?
     What plans do you have for helping?

2.   Is my child Hyperactive? Distractible? If yes,
     Why do you feel he or she is?
     If you are considering medication, which medication? How much?
     What does it do? For how long? What side-effects may be anticipated?
     (The issue of medication will be discussed in a different chapter)

3.   Does my child have emotional or social problems? If yes,
     What are they?
     Why do you think they exist? (Be sure the professionals distinguish between emotional problems that cause academic difficulties and emotional problems that are a consequence of academic difficulties.)

What do you recommend we do about them?

4. Do we have family problems to deal with? If yes,
   What are they?
   What do you suggest we do?
   If no one sees an adverse impact of problems on the marriage or siblings but you do, say so now and ask for help.

5. Who will coordinate all of these recommended actions and be sure that everyone involved communicates with each other?
   If no one is named, pick someone and ask if he or she will accept this role.

6. When should we meet again to assess progress and plan ahead?
   Don't leave without a firm date, or a firm date to set a date.

Preparing Your Child or Adolescent for an Evaluation

When an evaluation is in order, your child or adolescent must know why it is being done, who he or she will see, and what will be done. Be as honest and direct as possible. Acknowledge that she or he has been having problems at school (and possibly at home), and explain them as fully as necessary. Tell the youngster that he or she must be frustrated and unhappy. You, too, feel frustrated and unhappy. You want to try to understand just what the problems are and why they exist so that something can be done to correct them and make things better. The words you choose to get this across will depend on your son's or daughter's age and your style of relating to the child, but the message should not vary: We care about you; you are hurting; we must do something to help.

If possible, make a list of each person that the child will see. Identify who each is and what each will probably do. You might say the following:

Educational testing This is not like a school test. There may not be right or wrong answers. The test will help us understand how you learn best and where you have trouble learning. The results will help us plan a way to help you if you have learning problems.

Psychological testing The psychologist will talk with you and do tests. These tests will try to help us understand how you solve learning and life problems. Yes, an IQ test will be done to help us understand why you might be having difficulties with learning.

You might want to emphasize to the child that no one thinks he or she is retarded.

Mental-health evaluation No formal test will be done. A person will simply talk with you. He or she knows about learning difficulties and about the worries and problems that people who have such difficulties sometimes have.

You might want to add that you do not think the child is crazy. But you see that he or she is frustrated and/or unhappy and this specialist can help plan what to do about it. If the mental-health professional is a physician, either a general psychiatrist or a child psychiatrist, and your child is young, you might want to reassure your daughter or son that unlike the family doctor, this doctor will not give shots.

Special tests If special tests are to be done, brain wave studies, for example, ask the person who will be doing them to help you explain what will happen and why the studies are to be done.

Never surprise your child or adolescent by tricking him or her into going to see someone. Your youngster has a right to know what is going on and why. If your son or daughter refuses to participate in any part of the evaluation, ask a member of the team or the person he or she is to see how to approach this resistance.

After the Evaluation

Once you, the parents, understand the results and recommendations, you should see to it that the person who was evaluated also knows what they are. If you feel capable of sharing this information yourself, you might try it. Preferably, however, one of the professionals who participated in the evaluation should meet with the child or adolescent, review the findings, and outline the plans.

At some point the rest of the family should be fully informed. Sisters or brothers, and possibly significant grandparents, aunts, and uncles need to know what the results were and what plans have been made in order to give informed support to the treatment.

I cannot over-emphasize that the evaluation is only a start. You must follow up on every recommendation to make sure that everything agreed upon continues to be done. Even when the school has started a program for your child, you must monitor it to see that everything agreed upon is offered. Frequent contact is needed, and usually you must initiate it.

You must also be sure that everyone involved in the treatment process communicates with each other. The regular classroom teacher must know what the special educator is doing. The doctor prescribing medication must get feedback from you and from the school. And don't forget to talk about all of this with your son or daughter. How do they feel things are going? Their opinions are, perhaps, most critical of all.

If things do not get better or get worse, talk to the teacher or special educator. When a school year comes to an end, request a meeting to review progress and make plans for the next year.

Being a constant advocate is hard work. But no one can be as motivated and concerned as you, the parents. Your task is not only essential, it is unavoidable.

10

The Evaluation Procedures

Now that we have looked at the evaluation process in general, I would like to review each part of this process, focusing on particular types of studies and tests that are done. The more you know about these things, the more intelligent a consumer you can become.

The Educational Evaluation

The primary purpose of the educational evaluation is to identify your child's areas of learning strength and any learning weaknesses or disabilities. The major goal of such testing is to bring to light what can and should be done to intervene in these areas of weakness and to establish a special school program which can help the child to compensate for and master them.

The steps of this evaluation include the measurement of:

1. Intelligence
2. Achievement levels in school skill areas
3. Learning strengths and weaknesses

Intelligence

The first task is to assess a child's potential for learning. The IQ test which accomplishes this may be given by a trained special educator or by a psychologist.

The two most frequently given tests of intellectual ability are the Stanford-Binet and the Wechsler Intelligence tests. The Wechsler Tests come in three different units: the Wechsler Pre-School and Primary Scale of Intelligence (WPPSI), the Wechsler Intelligence Scale for Children (WISC), and the Wechsler Adult Intelligence Scale (WAIS). Several screening tests are also used to determine who might need more extensive studies. Each is timed so that a standardized score for the person's age can be determined.

1. *The Stanford-Binet Intelligence Scale* is for age 2 to adulthood. It emphasizes verbal responses more than nonverbal. Thus if a child was tested on the Stanford-Binet scale when a preschooler, then on the Wechsler scale several years later, the two IQ scores may not be comparable.

2. *The Wechsler Pre-School and Primary Scale of Intelligence* is for ages 4 to 6¹/₂ and measures verbal and nonverbal reasoning and perceptual motor abilities.

3. *The Wechsler Intelligence Scale for Children* is for ages 6 through 16 and measures general intelligence. Five parts measure verbal abilities and five parts measure nonverbal, or performance abilities. The scores on these two parts are combined to produce a full-scale score.

4. *The Wechsler Adult Intelligence Scale* tests verbal and nonverbal intelligence of adults aged 16 and over.

These intellectual assessment tests provide more than an IQ score. Equally important, the results assist in the diagnostic process. Children with learning disabilities will do well on the parts of the test that utilize their areas of strengths, but poorly on the parts that touch their areas of disabilities. When the differences in the subtest scores (called "subtest scatter") are compared with the rest of the results of the educational evaluation, the picture of the learning disabilities and the reasons for poor classroom performances become clearer. For people with learning disabilities, we cannot use the IQ test in isolation. The scores simply do not truly measure intelligence. The subtest scores do, however, help to identify areas of weakness and to suggest intellectual potential.

The Wechsler Intelligence Scale for Children (WISC) is used so frequently, and the subtest results provide such meaningful information, that we should look at this test in some detail.

The WISC has a *verbal* and a *performance*, or nonverbal, part. Each part has five subtests.

WISC Verbal Scale
Information test
Comprehension test
Similarities test
Arithmetic test
Vocabulary test
(A Digit-Span test can also be used)

WISC Performance Scale
Picture Arrangement test
Picture Completion test
Block Design test
Object Assembly test
Coding test
(A Maze test can also be used)

Each subtest measures a different area of intellectual functioning, each score being based on the expected normal performance for a person of similar age. Each area of function, and therefore each score, can be affected by learning disabilities.

Information (verbal)   This subtest measures the amount of general knowledge a person has acquired both in school and as a result of life experiences in the family or elsewhere. Children with learning disabilities who do poorly in school might have picked up a lot of general information outside of school and do well on this subtest.

Comprehension (verbal) This subtest measures abstract thinking and one's ability to comprehend concepts. This test may possibly measure basic native intelligence separate from learned knowledge.

Similarities (verbal) This subtest measures abstract thinking by asking how things are alike or different. This test, like comprehension, aims to measure basic native intelligence.

Arithmetic (verbal) This subtest measures one's numerical reasoning ability by using verbal problems, that is, story problems written out in words. Children who are below grade level in arithmetic may do poorly.

Vocabulary (verbal) This subtest requires a child to define or explain the words given. It measures general exposure to words as well as words learned in school.

Picture Completion Test (performance) This subtest requires the ability to analyze a total picture and identify what is missing. The child has to find the missing part and place it into the total picture.

Picture Arrangement Test (performance) This subtest requires the ability to pick up clues suggesting a necessary sequence of events. Pictures must be placed together to tell a coherent story.

Block Design (performance) With a set of blocks available, the child must look at a picture of a design, then put the blocks together to make that design. The child must analyze the whole complex picture, then break down the pattern into its parts so as to know which blocks to put where.

Object Assembly (performance) This subtest presents the parts of an object (e.g., a person) which the child must put together. This calls for abilities opposite to those needed for picture completion or block design. Here the parts must be analyzed and put into a whole.

Coding (performance) A code is given (e.g., $2 = *$), then a sequence is given. The child must use the code to decode the sequence. For example, the alphabet might be listed, A through Z. Next to each is a symbol. Then, a message is written using the symbols. This message must be decoded using the code provided.

Each subtest requires different abilities and accomplishments. Some require auditory skills, others test verbal skills. Some require basic knowledge, and others test acquired knowledge. This acquired knowledge might be learned in school or outside of school. Some subtests require short-term memory, integration, or abstraction. Some require language, visual motor skills, gross motor skills, or fine motor skills.

Children with learning disabilities may do well on those subtests where their problems do not interfere, and their scores in these areas should suggest their intellectual potential. They usually do not do as well on those subtests which demand performance in their area of disability. These scores, perhaps, best reflect how the child is performing in the classroom.

For example, suppose twelve-year-old Tom has good auditory perception, auditory sequencing, auditory abstraction, auditory memory, and language skills. But Tom also has visual perceptual, visual sequencing, visual abstraction, visual memory, fine motor, and visual motor disabilities. He has been in special education classes. His WISC might read:

Verbal IQ 128
Performance IQ 88
Full Scale IQ 108

To say that Tom is of average intelligence (IQ 108) is misleading and incorrect. What can be said, perhaps, is that he shows evidence of superior intelligence based on test scores where he has no disability (verbal). He is bright, but frustrated in school because of his disabilities. In most school efforts requiring visual and motor skills, he probably performs at a below average level.

Let me go through Tom's test results to illustrate how to understand the scores. The numbers are his subtest scores. They are averaged and converted, using a standard chart, to provide an IQ score.

TEST AND SCORE		POSSIBLE MEANING
Verbal Tests		These are in areas of his learning strengths.
Information	14	Suggests a child of superior intelligence who is learning through school and general life experiences.
Similarities	15	Suggests a child of superior intelligence with good reasoning and abstraction abilities.
Arithmetic	9	Suggests that the level of math learned in special-education programs was not at the expected 6th-grade level.
Vocabulary	17	Suggests a child of superior intelligence who is learning through school and general life experiences.
Comprehension	13	Suggests a child of high-average to superior intelligence.

His Verbal IQ score is 128, in the superior range. Yet note how his lower math score (due to his special-education classes), when averaged with the others, lowers his IQ score.

TEST AND SCORE	POSSIBLE MEANING
Performance Tests	These are in areas of his learning weaknesses.
Picture Completion 8	Probably his visual perception and visual motor problems interfered with this task. He scores in the low-average range.
Picture Arrangement 10	This is an average score; yet, for a boy of his ability, it would be seen as underperformance. Probably his visual perception and sequencing problems interfered.
Block Design 7	This low-average to borderline score possibly reflects his visual perception, visual memory, and visual motor problems, plus his anxiety with timed tests.
Object Assembly 10	This is an average score but an under performance for him. The same learning disabilities probably interfered.
Coding 3	The anxiety plus visual perception, visual memory, and visual motor tasks result in a score in the retarded range.

His Performance IQ scores at 88, the low-average range. Perhaps this score reflects his level of performance in the classroom with timed and written tests. It in no way reflects his level of intelligence.

The Full Scale IQ scores at 108, average. In no way does this truly reflect his intelligence.

These scores suggest a boy of superior intellectual ability who has learning disabilities that interfere with certain test performances, resulting in lower scores on some subtests. These lower scores suggest the types of problems he might have in school. The difference between his intellectual ability and his school performance may explain his frustrations and poor self-image.

Never let someone give you only an IQ score. You must look at the full test and the scores on each part. To say that Tom was of average intelligence (IQ 108) would be inaccurate. For the school to design an appropriate program for him based on the average IQ rather than based on his superior IQ potential would be equally wrong. Only a full understanding of all the test results and their meaning can lead to a program interpretation and appropriate program planning.

Achievement Levels

Once IQ is measured and intellectual potential known, it is necessary to compare this with the true performance. Standardized achievement tests are given by the special-education person to measure where the child or adolescent is performing in different skill areas. The results may be presented either in terms of grade-level performance or in terms of percentile level for one's age—that is, where your child is performing either compared to all other children in his or her grade or compared to those at his or her age. There are several such tests, among which some of the more commonly used are:

> *Metropolitan Achievement Tests* Used for grades 1 through 8, this test is given to a group of children at the same time. It assesses levels of achievement in a wide range of language and arithmetic skills.
> *Peabody Individual Achievement Test* This test is used for ages 5 to adulthood to measure general academic achievement in reading mechanics and comprehension, spelling, math, and general knowledge.
> *Stanford Diagnostic Achievement Tests* Used for grades 1 through 12 to assess mathematics and reading skills, this test also provides instructional objectives and suggestions for teaching.
> *Wide-Range Achievement Tests* Used from kindergarten through college, this test covers oral reading, spelling, and arithmetic computation. Scores are by grade level for each skill.
> *Woodcock-Johnson Psychoeducational Battery, Tests of Academic Achievement and Interest* Used from preschool through adult level to measure achievement in reading, math, written language, and general knowledge, these tests also assess the level of academic versus nonacademic accomplishments.

Specific achievement tests relating to reading might be used. The results of these tests may be expressed as a grade equivalent or as a percentile ranking. Such tests are also used to assess strengths and weaknesses in order to plan remedial instruction. Some of these tests include:

> *Durrell Analysis of Reading Difficulty* Used for nonreaders through 6th-grade levels, this test includes oral and silent reading and

listening comprehension, as well as word-recognition, word-analysis, and supplemental tests of visual and auditory skills needed for reading.

Gates-MacGinitie Reading Tests Used for individuals or a group and for grades 1 through 12, it measures vocabulary and comprehension.

Gates-McKillop Reading Diagnostic Test This test measures reading skills, including sight vocabulary, oral phonetic relationships, paragraphs (i.e., reading aloud), and spelling in nonreaders and readers.

Gray Oral Reading Test Although it measures oral-reading fluency based on speed and accuracy, this test does not measure comprehension.

Other special tests cover spelling and written language, arithmetic, and oral language.

Learning Strengths and Disabilities

If a discrepancy exists between a person's intellectual ability and his or her performance level, one must find out why. Several broad-based tests assess all aspects of learning, looking at the input, integration, memory, and output skills that I discussed earlier. Several of these general tests are:

Detroit Tests of Learning Aptitude
Illinois Test of Psycholinguistic Abilities
McCarthy Scales of Children's Abilities
Slingerland Screening Tests for Identifying
    Children with Specific Language Disabilities

If the general tests reveal areas of disability, special tests that focus on these disabilities—auditory perception, visual perception, visual-motor integration, memory, language, and motor development—may also be given. In addition, a speech and language therapist, or an occupational therapist may participate in expanding the educational evaluation.

The completed evaluation should point clearly to areas of learning disability as well as those of learning ability. It should contain recommendations for an academic program, including the type of placement needed and suggestions for the necessary educational intervention. Strategies to enhance learning should also be identified.

The Psychiatric Evaluation

The psychiatric evaluation focuses on functioning at several levels and focuses on the interrelationships among them. The *intrapsychic assessment* notes the issues or conflicts the child or adolescent is currently facing and the coping techniques he or she has called into play in order to deal with them. The clinician also notes whether these behaviors are age-appropriate or not.

The *interpersonal assessment* focuses on the child's style of interacting with parents, other adults, siblings, and peers.

A *behavioral assessment* tries to clarify which behaviors the child is hanging onto because they have become learned patterns of behavior through selective rewards (reinforcement) or nonrewards by parents or others.

The *systems assessment* focuses on the child's roles in the family, as well as in other systems—the school, or the neighborhood, for example. The clinician determines how the roles that the child plays in one system influence or interact with the roles he or she plays in other systems. Are the behaviors observed a reflection of family stress or a cause that contributes to family stress?

The evaluation work may take place in the mental health professional's office, with the child, the parents, and/or the family. If direct observation of the school experience is not possible, teachers' reports will be examined and taken into account.

If, at the end of the evaluation, the clinician concludes that the child's emotional, social, or family difficulties either reflect or are caused by her or his learning disabilities, a treatment strategy should be suggested. If the problems are due to frustrations, failures, and school stress, no treatment may be started until the remedial educational strategies are in place. Then, if the child's problem behaviors persist, therapeutic help may begin.

These emotional, social, or family problems may have started as a consequence of learning disabilities. If now they seem so ingrained that they have a life of their own, the clinician may recommend individual, group, behavioral, or family therapy, or some combination of these. I cover these treatments in more detail in Chapter 13.

The Medical Evaluation

Your family physician must make sure that the child has no physical difficulties. Other professionals will examine him or her if any hearing, vision, or eye-muscle imbalance difficulties are suspected. A neurological evaluation may be requested because of some concern with the child's behavior or because the school requires it.

If the history or observational data suggest that a seizure has occurred, an electroencephalogram (EEG) is done. Several types of seizures are possible. *Grand mal* seizures (generally called "epilepsy") are characterized by major convulsions, with intermittent spasms of all the body muscles, followed by a jerking motion of these muscles. After the seizure the child is asleep or lethargic. When he or she wakes up, the child is confused, disoriented, and has no memory of the event. During a grand mal seizure some people lose bladder or bowel control. Many report a brief sensory experience, or "aura," prior to the seizure. *Petit mal* seizures are brief attacks, with momentary loss of consciousness often associated with symmetrical jerking movements of the eyelids or some other part of the body. Sometimes no muscle activity occurs, just the brief loss of consciousness. Once the episode ends, the child is alert and has no memory loss except for the short span of the seizure. *Psychomotor seizures* are accompanied by attacks of a wide variety of confused behaviors. Explosive, aggressive actions may occur. The sufferer is confused and disoriented after the episode. Or a child may have a *focal seizure*, which is characterized by convulsions confined to a single limb or muscle group, or to a specific type of sensory disturbance.

Whatever the malfunction, the EEG should detect the problem and provide valuable diagnostic information.

After the Evaluation: A Final Note

Once again, let me stress that you must learn everything you can about the evaluation. And you must share these facts with the son or daughter who has had the tests as well as with the rest of the family.

One final comment. After you have talked with the person

coordinating the evaluation, *ask for copies of each report as well as a summary of the full evaluation.* Read all of these reports and be sure you understand what they say. If you don't understand anything, be assertive and ask questions.

Keep a file of all the evaluations that are made. They will be useful in the future when reevaluations may be needed.

Part Four

Treatment

11

___

Your Role in the Treatment for the Learning Disabilities

Nowhere is understanding your total child in his or her total environment more important than when you are dealing with learning disabilities. As I have been saying over and over, they do not just interfere with reading, writing, and arithmetic; they interfere with all aspects of life—at home, in the neighborhood, at church and in religious classes, in sports, at clubs and other organized activities—in short, everyplace. Wherever your son or daughter goes, you must be an advocate for making the most of his or her strengths. You must see to it that your child has as many positive experiences as possible. How do you build on the child's strengths and minimize the weaknesses? Who can work with you at school, at home, and outside of the home?

To start, do you know where your child or adolescent's learning disabilities and learning strengths are? If not, ask to meet with the special-education team at your school or, if the evaluations were not done by the school, with the special educator who did the testing. You might look back over the material we covered in the chapters on specific learning disabilities and on evaluation and any notes you have made on your daughter's or son's evaluation. Then get yourself to the school and begin asking for details and any reports of progress.

Because your child spends so much time at school, and because that is usually where special-education programs are put into effect, I shall focus first on the treatment of learning disabilities in the school environment.

The School Environment

Ideally your school system is as concerned as you are about developing the necessary help and the proper program for your child. If not, you may need to push for what you need. (I discuss how to be such an advocate more fully in Chapter 15 on legal issues.)

Depending on the school's facilities, budget, and approach to the problem, your son or daughter will be placed either in a special-education classroom or in a special resource room for part of the day. Or the child may be in a regular classroom but also receive supplemental special-educational tutoring. Whatever the program, you must find out what is to be accomplished and if the special-classroom or resource-room teacher or tutor is fully trained in special education.

Finding an Appropriate School Program

If the school does not provide these resources, or if you cannot get what you need from the school, you may be able to provide back-up help for your child or adolescent by hiring a private special-education tutor for sessions once or several times a week. If you make arrangements like this, it is absolutely essential that this tutor communicate with the child's classroom teachers. If supplemental private tutoring is not sufficient to handle the problem, you may need to consider a private school placement.

Many cities have private special-education schools that are staffed and programmed especially for children or adolescents with learning disabilities. In some states, if a public school cannot provide an appropriate program, the school district will refer your son or daughter to a private special-education school which has the facilities and services that the child needs. Your school's special-education department can give you a list of the private programs

available in your area. You can also order directories of such schools
from:

1. The Director for Exceptional Children
    Porter Sargent Publishers, Inc.
    11 Beacon Street
    Boston, Massachusetts 02108

2. Director of Facilities and Services for the Learning-Disabled
    Academic Therapy Publication
    20 Commercial Boulevard
    Novato, California 94947

Remember that there is nothing magical about a private school.
Not just any private school will do, either. A private school that
provides general education may turn out to cause more stress for
the child than your public school. You may get smaller classes and
more structure, but with it may come an excessive emphasis on
grades and college preparation, and, with that, intense competition
among the students.

A school that is designed and staffed to work exclusively with
people who have learning disabilities is probably what you want.
Know what you are getting. Talk to parents of children at the
private school about academic demands, number of homework
hours, and flexibility. Ask other parents of children with learning
disabilities for advice about what to do and what not to do, and
weigh their experiences when you make your choices. (You can
meet such parents through your local chapter of The Association
for Children with Learning Disabilities—see Appendix for address.)

If you find that you cannot get the appropriate special-educational help anywhere, you may have to consider a boarding school.
To me, this is always the last choice, and you should consider it
only if it is absolutely necessary. Boarding schools can be excellent,
and some have special programs for those with learning disabilities.
But if your son or daughter is to live away from home, you must
weigh the loss of the security and strength that the family provides
against whatever your child will gain from the programs at the
facility.

Still, if you cannot find any local programs tailored to help with
learning disabilities, or if your child's behavior at school or at home
is so problematic that you must consider a boarding school or

residential treatment center, get the best help you can in selecting a good one, one that will work for your child.

Three Program Levels

Three kinds of programs are generally available in the public schools or in private special-education schools. Which one you select will depend on the degree of your child's disabilities, his or her level of current academic performance, the availability of programs, and, of course, the advice of the specialists caring for your child.

The best program offers what the child needs academically and behaviorally in the *least restrictive environment* possible. This judgment has to be made for each child individually. The least restrictive environment is not necessarily the program closest to a regular program. For some children and adolescents, the least restrictive environment that will do the job might be the most restrictive environment available. For example, a child with multiple learning disabilities who is several years behind in basic skills might feel most relaxed and safe in a small, self-contained, special-education classroom. The freedom and rough-and-tumble of a regular classroom might so overwhelm the child that his or her involvement would be completely inhibited.

If he or she can handle it, your son or daughter could go into a regular classroom program with a daily half-hour or hour of supplemental special-education help. This is the *first*, or *lightest level*. For a program like this to work, the special-education people must communicate actively with the classroom teachers. I have been surprised at how often the classroom teacher has no idea what goes on in the "tutoring." He or she may even continue to expect too much or penalize the child because of his or her learning problems. Find out what is going on by talking to both teachers. If they are not communicating, push for it.

Another concern is that you monitor the program carefully. Schools may promise the world in the fall. But somehow the hour a day slowly decreases to half an hour or even less. Don't let this happen without your knowledge and concurrence. Ask your child from time to time how often he or she sees the special help teacher and for how long. If the time is less than was promised, call up and find out what's going on and why.

The program at the *second level* of intensity is often called "mainstreaming." The child or adolescent is assigned basically to a resource room staffed with special educators, then "mainstreamed" into regular classroom programs for as much of the day as he or she can handle. At first, this might be just gym class, music, or art. Later, it might include English, science, or math. As with the supplemental-help model, however, it is critical that the resource-room special educators communicate with regular classroom teachers. Your role in seeing that this happens looms just as large, too.

If a yet more intensive, *third-level program* is needed, your son or daughter might be assigned fulltime to a self-contained class-room. Such a program is designed and staffed exclusively for learning disabled children or adolescents. Classes usually have no more than eight to twelve students and are run by a certified special-education teacher and an aide.

Whichever program your child or adolescent goes into, remember that no matter how sincere and cooperative the school may be, your concerns are greater. Keep informed. Monitor what is done. Don't be afraid to ask if the teacher is trained and certified in special education. If the school does not plan occasional conferences to give progress reports, request one, and then request others at reasonable intervals. If you have not heard from the school by early spring about planning for next year's placement, call and ask for a meeting.

The Regular Classroom Teacher

If your son or daughter is in the regular classroom for all or part of the day, what should you expect of the regular classroom teacher? He or she must at least be knowledgeable about your child's particular pattern of learning disabilities and abilities. The classroom teacher may not have the time or the training to offer remedial therapy. The special educators can handle this. But the classroom teacher can only reach your child by utilizing his or her strengths while understanding or compensating for the weaknesses.

If a child had a congenitally deformed leg, no teacher would expect him or her to run on the playground as well as the other children. If a child were blind, no teacher would hand him or her a printed speller to read. If a child were deaf, no teacher would ask him or her to sound out a word. But the child with learning disabilities has invisible handicaps, hard to see and therefore easy to forget. Unless the classroom teacher remains constantly aware of them, she or he may very well make equally unrealistic demands.

By the same token, the sensitive, well-informed classroom teacher can do much to help your child. If the teacher knows that the child has auditory perceptual problems, for example, he or she can try a multisensory approach. While helping with the phonics, an approach that requires visual and tactile activities along with sound inputs can be used. If a child has visual motor and fine motor problems, he or she might not have to write an answer on the board but could be called on to answer the question verbally. If a child has a demand language disability, the teacher should call on him or her only if the child volunteers or if the child initiates the conversation, but never ask the child to answer unexpectedly. This child, though, could write an answer on the board.

If a child has written language disabilities, the school could introduce typing (a gross motor skill) or allow the use of a tape recorder. While other children write their class or homework assignments, this child could speak into a tape recorder. If the child does write an assignment, the emphasis should be on the content, not the spelling or handwriting, and the teacher might allow more time to complete it.

In planning activities during lunch or playtime, knowing the child's abilities and disabilities allows the teacher to set up situations and suggest activities that the child can handle and, one would hope, succeed in.

The regular classroom can be a positive learning place where the child can succeed, build a positive self-image, and feel good about himself or herself. Or it can be a negative place where the child experiences frustration and failure, often leading to acting-out behavior. To create positive experiences, the classroom teacher must know what he or she is dealing with and must make that extra creative effort.

Homework

What about homework? Who is responsible for what?

If you find yourself teaching your child how to do his or her homework or doing the work yourself because the child doesn't know how and "it must be done," or if your child can whine and cry, blackmailing you into doing the work, something is wrong. If you find yourself in situations like these, ask for a conference and discuss the problems.

All youngsters need help from time to time with their homework. Those with learning disabilities may need extra assistance. I believe, however, that the main role for parents is to help their children feel good about themselves. This means helping them to build a good self-image, encouraging their feelings of acceptance, seeing that they feel loved. For some children and adolescents, being able to work with their parents on schoolwork is a positive and sought after experience. Some however, take advantage of the situation, and this ultimately erodes the child's self-esteem. Others don't like to expose their weaknesses or reveal their problems and resist help or say they don't have any homework. If you find yourself wondering about such a problem, you may want to talk to your child's teachers and to your son or daughter about it. Let the teachers help you figure out how much help should be needed. Don't let your child browbeat or nag you into doing her or his work.

I sometimes hear parents complain that a child worked for two or three hours on a homework assignment which the teacher said should take fifteen minutes. If you are facing such a discrepancy, explore the problem with the teacher. Are the child's poor handwriting skills making the task too difficult? Does the child understand the assignment? Are modifications in the length of the assignment or in the teacher's expectations in general needed?

You can do some things to help with the process of doing homework and with preparation for school that do not require sitting down and doing the child's work.

1. Help your child or adolescent to organize materials for school. The youngster may be keeping English papers in the math book or today's work with old returned papers. Work with your daughter or son to set up a system and ask the teacher to help with it.

2. Some youngsters have difficulty with lockers. They lose their keys or forget their combinations. Or they lose whatever they are carrying around. Maybe it would be better to carry everything in a big gym bag or back pack. Get one with compartments so that it can be organized more easily.

3. Make sure the child understands homework instructions. Memory problems, poor handwriting, or Distractibility may result in an incomplete or incorrect idea of what to do at home. The youngster may cover this up by saying there is no homework or may do only part of the task because she or he didn't understand the full assignment. Suppose the teacher put a spelling list or homework assignment on the board. If the child copies it down wrong,

it will be done wrong. Ask each teacher to be sure that your son or daughter understands the assignment and has it correct at the end of class. If the assignment is written on the board, ask if it can be given to your child on a piece of paper that he or she can bring home.

4. If you feel that too much homework is being assigned, meet with the teacher or team of teachers. Discuss what you feel your child can handle. Work out a plan before the overload frustrates the child and turns him or her off completely.

5. Distraction may interfere with successful concentration on homework assignments. Help find a quiet, uncluttered area with few distractions. Some children may find music as a background helpful because it blocks out other distractions.

6. You may find that it helps to set aside a specific time each day or on weekends for doing homework. With older children it might be better to give them less structure and more control of their own time. "You can do your homework anytime after you get home, but you can't watch TV until it's done."

7. At bedtime you might help your daughter or son get ready for the next day. Are all the necessary books and papers in the school bag? Check for the gym bag, special clothes, lunch money, anything unusual for a special project. Such planning cuts down on the confusion in the morning and helps to assure that nothing is forgotten.

If your child seems to have little or no homework while his or her teachers complain that the child doesn't turn in work or comes to class unprepared, ask for a conference with the teachers *and* your child. Try to set up a plan. The teacher might send home a list of homework requirements each day. Before bedtime, you check the list to see if it all has been done. Or you might ask the school to help you negotiate the problem. If work is not done, the child misses recess or lunch or stays after school. Don't be put into the role of playing policeman at home if it makes a constant struggle or fight of your evening. Ask the school to assist in the responsibility for following up on homework assignments.

The Home Environment

You want to help all of your children to grow up with a positive self-image and with confidence. This is hard enough to do, but it requires even greater effort if your son or daughter has learning disabilities. Don't excuse this child from chores, even though that might be the easy way out. A double standard for this child and the other children in the family sends the nonverbal message that you too think that the learning disabled child is inadequate. Building on your knowledge of what the child can and cannot do, try to select tasks and activities that she or he is most likely to succeed at. This success builds confidence, and with that confidence comes increasing social acceptance.

Let's discuss home first, then the neighborhood, clubs, and other activities. I can't give you a ready-made program, but I can suggest an approach—a way of thinking and problem-solving.

Your son or daughter's learning disabilities will be quite apparent at home. Tell the child clearly that you understand, and make sure the child hears and believes you. Reassure your daughter or son that you are glad that she or he is getting help. Ask for the child's own advice on how you can help best. In talking to a child with an auditory figure-ground problem—that is, difficulty selecting what sounds to focus on—you may need to establish eye contact before speaking. Go into the room where the child is and call out his or her name. Speak to the child only after she or he has looked up. If your child has difficulty with sequencing—that is, getting the steps of a task in the right order—help the child get started. Don't do the job for the child, but help him or her get organized. If you want the table set, for instance, put a sample setting down (plate here, fork, knife, and spoon there, glass here). If your child has trouble dressing in the morning because it's hard to figure out what goes first, maybe you can place the clothes out on the bed in sequence. If your child has fine motor problems and difficulty with buttons or shoe laces, try slip-over tops or loafers. You can't avoid every area of difficulty, but you can make the most of what the child can do independently.

Make a list of the areas in which the child is strong and weak. Next to each strength, write out all of the things he or she is capable of doing. Next to the weaknesses, write out all of the things that you notice that a disability interferes with. Then think creatively about what you could do to build on the child's strengths while helping to compensate for weaknesses. For example, what household chores can the child do? If gross motor problems result in frequent accidents while the child takes out the trash, can some other tasks be assigned? Possibly the counselor or someone else on the special-education staff at school can help you with this. One rule I find helpful is this: *If you find yourself struggling to decide whether your child can or cannot do something because of a disability, assume that he or she can do it and insist on it.* If the child succeeds, great! If she or he continues to have problems, you can always pull back. The question is not whether he or she can do a task. The question is *how* he or she can do the task.

If you would like to take an active part in helping your child work on his or her areas of disability, consider using normal household activities to reinforce learning. Again, I cannot write out a recipe for helping your child or adolescent. I can only suggest a way of thinking. Many kitchen activities, for instance, require reading, measuring, counting, and following instructions. These provide good practice in sequencing. Chopping and stirring make good gross motor exercises. If you want to improve auditory memory, take the child shopping with you. At first, while near the correct shelf, ask the child to pick up one item, a can of peas, let's say. Later, make it two or three items. Still later, make it an item an aisle over, then two aisles. If you want to work actively with your child in this fashion, no doubt you can think of many other situations that come up in your daily life where your child can practice the skills she or he lacks.

The same techniques can be applied outside the home in sports, at clubs, and in other activities. Each sport requires different strengths. If your son or daughter has sequencing, fine motor, and visual motor disabilities, games with elaborate rules, or those which require skills, like baseball and basketball, will be difficult. The child's poor performance also adds to social and peer problems. But let us say that he or she has good gross motor strengths. Try swimming, diving, soccer, horseback riding, skiing, bowling, or certain field and track events, all of which rely on gross motor abilities. The same ten-year-old who stopped playing baseball because he could not catch, throw, or hit well, and who did no better at basketball, might do very well in soccer or become an excellent swimmer. Let the child find success and peer acceptance with these sports.

Some children find all sports difficult. But it might be possible to improve some of the required skills through practice. Most of the kids his or her own age won't take the time or have the patience to help. But a parent or an older brother or sister can go into the yard, or anyplace else where the other kids won't see, and practice catching, throwing, or hitting.

Because of the difficulty following directions or because they simply play so badly, some children never learn the basic rules of a game. Once again, you or someone in the family may need to sit down and teach the child how to play baseball, or hopscotch, from the ground up, going back over the rules until the child catches on.

You can use this approach with all of the child's outside activities. Build on strengths: Don't magnify weaknesses. Picture a ten-year-old with fine motor, sequencing, and visual motor disabilities at a Cub Scout or an Indian Princess meeting. Everyone is cutting out pumpkins, or turkeys, or whatever, and your child's cutouts are total failures. Everybody laughs at them. Another failure, and the child doesn't want to go to anymore meetings. But if the activity leaders had known what the child couldn't do, they could have tapped the gross motor abilities the child does have. He or she could hand out the paper, squirt the glue, or smear the paste. Failure could be turned into success. Similarly, on parent night, your daughter shouldn't have to demonstrate knot tying. But she could march in carrying the flag.

When such children go to the local youth center, don't let them wander around and select what they want to do at random. Whether they should be in arts and crafts or photography depends on what they are able to do reasonably well. Crafts require good visual perception and eye-hand coordination; many aspects of photography involve gross motor skills. Plan ahead for those occasions. And use the club, group, or activities leaders as extensions of yourself. Help them to understand what you want to accomplish beforehand. They can help you only if you have advocated your own cause.

Make sure such people understand that your child does not always hear every instruction given; they must know in advance to check with the child and repeat things if necessary. Your child may appear quiet or indifferent because language does not come easily. Tell this to the people in charge. You may have to explain the whole thing: your child is not retarded, bad, or lazy. The disability is simply invisible. You can and must make the instructor or activity leader sensitive to your child's special needs. The same advice holds for Sunday school and religious-education programs.

Be sure that the staff knows all about the child so that they can work with you in designing appropriate classroom and activity programs.

Choosing a camp, whether day or sleep-away, requires the same attention. You may need to consider a camp designed for children with special needs, or you might be able to use a carefully selected regular camp. Think about whether your child can handle a large or small camp. What strengths and abilities does the child have, and how do you match them with the offerings of a camp? Some camps focus on drama or arts and crafts. Are these activities that will build on your son's strengths or will he sustain more damage because he looks foolish? Some camps are sports-oriented and competitive. Woe to the girl who drops a ball and causes her cabin to lose the game! But there are camps that do focus on noncompetitive activities or on gross motor sports. Your clumsy, nonathletic son or daughter might do very well at a camp that focuses on horseback riding or on waterfront activities. Swimming, rowing, sailing, all are gross motor activities.

Before selecting a camp, talk with the director at length. Is that person flexible? Can she or he describe programs that might work for your particular child? Don't hesitate to educate the counselors, either. They will appreciate the information, and your son or daughter will undoubtedly benefit from the understanding of such important people.

In Summary

In this chapter I have tried to illustrate a style of thinking and problem-solving. The specific examples may or may not fit your particular child or adolescent, but the general principles apply to every case.

It is work. You must learn more about your youngster than you may have imagined possible. You must be creative. Yes, it is a lot of extra effort. But if you don't do it, who will?

12

Treatment for Hyperactivity and Distractibility

I have already described the possible causes of overactive or distractible behavior. You will recall that the Hyperactivity and/or Distractibility found in some learning disabled children and adolescents appears not to be due to anxiety or depression, but rather to a neurological difficulty. Current research suggests that this difficulty occurs in a part of the brain stem called the "ascending reticular activating system." It appears to relate to a deficit in a type of chemical, called a "neurotransmitter," that transmits impulses from one brain cell to another. The specific chemical may be norepinephrine or one of its breakdown products, dopa or dopamine.

If a child or adolescent is diagnosed as having this neurologically based Hyperactivity or Distractibility, several kinds of help are available. The youngster may need structure and a quieter or calmer environment. For some, a behavioral modification program may lessen the activity level or distractibility. For most, a medication will be prescribed. This type of medication is called a "psychostimulant" because in most people it stimulates the brain.

In 1937, a physician named Charles Bradley noted that these psychostimulants appeared to calm down some children who were

135

hyperactive. Since 1937, many studies have confirmed this observation. It has also been shown that medications, such as barbiturates, that depress brain function appear to increase the activity level in many of these same children.

We do not yet know why a brain stimulant calms these children while a brain depressant stimulates them. Possibly the system in the brain stem that controls muscle-activity level and sensory input into the brain is functioning so poorly that any medication which stimulates this area causes it to function better, resulting in less muscle activity and more control over sensory input into the brain. Thus, the person becomes less active and less distractible. Conversely, any medication that sedates this area of the brain causes it to function even less well, resulting in an increase in muscle activity and less control over sensory input into the brain. Contrary to normal expectation, the person becomes even more active and more distractible. Although we do not know precisely how these medications work, they do appear to compensate for a chemical imbalance that may occur in Hyperactive or Distractible children.

When a child or adolescent diagnosed as Hyperactive or Distractible is placed on a psychostimulant, we expect to find a decrease in muscle activity, resulting in a calmer child, and a decrease in distractibility, resulting in an increased attention span. Psychostimulants do not cause any improvement in anxiety-caused hyperactivity, nor do they cure the learning disabilities, although motor performance in some children may improve. Nor do they cure emotional, social, or family problems, although they do lessen some of the behaviors that cause such problems.

The Psychostimulants

The three commonly used psychostimulants are Ritalin (generic name: methylphenidate), Dexedrine (generic name: dextroamphetamine), and Cylert (generic name: pemoline).

Ritalin comes in three strengths, 5, 10, and 20 milligrams (abbreviated mg). The usual dosage is 5 to 15 mg three times a day, although some children may take up to 20 mg four times a day. It is also available in a 20 mg long-acting form, called Ritalin SR.

Dexedrine comes in liquid form, in 5 and 10 mg tablets, and in 5, 10, and 15 mg, 12-hour-acting "Spansules." The usual dosage is 5 or 10 mg two or three times a day, but more may be needed. Once a dosage pattern is established, one 12-hour, timed-release spansule in the morning may be considered. It lasts all day and avoids the need for additional pills.

Cylert is a long-acting medication, but several weeks may go by before its effects are noticed. It comes in 18.75, 37.5, and 75 mg tablets, and in a 37.5 mg chewable tablet.

Before I go into detail, I would like to spell out for you the general questions I shall answer. First, if your child is on a psychostimulant, should you discuss this with your family doctor and the child's classroom teachers? The answer is emphatically yes! Be sure every pertinent bit of information is communicated.

How much medication, when, and in what dosage is medication needed? You should be sure that your son or daughter is on as much medication as he or she needs *but no more*. Your physician should let you assist in monitoring the dosage, and I'll explain how you do this.

What are the possible side-effects of these drugs, and what do you do if they appear? I'll discuss this fully.

Finally, what should you do if your son or daughter resists taking the medicine? I'll suggest ideas. As with everything else, to be an assertive advocate, you must be an informed consumer.

Medication Dosage and Schedule

How much medication is needed?

The amount of medication needed must be determined by trying different dosages until an optimal level of the child's functioning is reached. One cannot predict the correct dosage in advance. Some children and adolescents metabolize the drugs more quickly and so need higher dosages than others. A child who needs 20 mg three times a day is not necessarily more disabled than a child who needs only 5 mg three times a day. The different dosage may only reflect the fact that the first child metabolizes the drug faster than the second.

When should the medication be used?

I must emphasize that Hyperactivity and/or Distractibility are not only school disabilities—they are life disabilities. They are behaviors that interfere with every aspect of family and social life. If a child responds positively to these medications, he or she should be on medication all day every day, not just during school hours. It is just as important for a child to sit calmly and pay attention at the dinner table or while playing with a friend as it is to function in class.

This is an important point. Some physicians still feel that the child should be on medication only during school hours. This model leaves the child off of medication during after-school and evening hours, weekends, and summers. The Hyperactive and/or Distractible child who responds positively to medication needs the medication to help with better function during all hours, not just during school hours. It is hardly fair to keep the child off medication during times when he or she wants—and needs—to relax, to relate, and to function casually and socially at dinner with the family, watching television with brothers and sisters, at Cub Scout meetings, Sunday school, or summer camp with friends. If your physician has your child or adolescent on medication during school hours only and if you notice the Hyperactive or Distractible behavior in the later afternoon, evenings, and on weekends, request that the dosage be expanded to cover these hours.

Can the dosage be varied depending on need?

Yes it can. Short-acting medications (Ritalin, Dexedrine) start to work in twenty to forty minutes and last three to five hours. They do not cure the problems, they only compensate for them while the drug is in effect. They do not accumulate, so after the medication wears off, the child is right back at the mercy of his or her previous Hyperactivity or Distractibility. Knowing this, and with your physician's permission, you can add to or subtract from the usual dosage pattern to fit the child's activities. For example, if your daughter takes 5 mg at 8:00 A.M., noon, and 4:00 P.M. and she has a Scout meeting or company is coming over, you may need to give her an extra 5 mg at 4:00 P.M., or 5 mg more at 6:00 P.M. If you are at the beach or the park and you feel that your son can run more freely than usual with little demand for carefully controlled behavior, you might skip the 4:00 P.M. dose. Think in four-hour units and learn what dosage works best for your child on what occasions. You can learn to orchestrate these medications very nicely after careful observation.

Possible Side-Effects

The psychostimulants have been used safely and effectively since the late 1930s. They do not make children or adolescents prone to drug dependence or more likely to use drugs inappropriately. Studies suggest quite the opposite: The children are apt to be more respectful of medication and less likely to abuse drugs. Your physician should discuss the possible side-effects of any course of medication with you. Let me review some of these effects and suggest approaches to dealing with them.

First is the question of height. A study done several years ago suggested that children who remained on psychostimulants for several consecutive years were 1 to 2 inches shorter than would otherwise have been expected. Since the study, several others were done that did not confirm these results. Other studies suggest that the hormone controlling growth is mainly released at night, when the child is off of medication. Perhaps the best comment is that at this time the research findings do not suggest that children on psychostimulants have a suppression of growth.

The psychostimulants may produce a loss of appetite, called "anorexia," and this can be a problem. This appetite loss may disappear after two or three weeks, but if it persists and the child starts losing weight, the dosage may have to be changed or a different medication prescribed.

You may also worry about nutrition, however, and the child's erratic eating habits may disrupt family routines. The medication may decrease appetite, and, like you if you are not very hungry, your child may become very picky about what he or she will eat. Or the child may prefer candy and snacks, eating little at the table during major meals. First, try to make snacks or desserts depend on whether or not the child eats the meal. Then, too, with your doctor's permission, you can vary the times for giving the medication. Give the first dose at breakfast—it won't start to work fast enough to affect the appetite. Lunch may be a loser. But if you can delay the afternoon dose until almost dinner time, your son or daughter may still have an appetite at meal time.

Some children have difficulty falling asleep and may lie in bed tossing restlessly for hours. Like the appetite problems, this effect may disappear during the first month of medication. With some children, the sleeplessness is a legitimate result of the psychostimulant, and it becomes necessary to discontinue the mid- or late-afternoon dose. With other children, the sleeplessness is not due to the medication but rather to the rebound effect of being off the medication. That is, a child on a three-times-a-day schedule is under the effect of the medication from morning until about four hours after the last dose. When the medication wears off, at 8 or 9 P.M., the child rebounds to his usual level of hyperactivity—or higher. The result is increased animation and restlessness at bedtime. The child is put to bed at 9 or 9:30, but simply can't unwind. For this child, an additional dose of the stimulant at about 8 P.M. may eliminate the difficulty with sleep. Stopping the afternoon dose helps in some cases; adding a bedtime dose helps in others. The two possible causes for sleeplessness are difficult to differentiate, and often a trial dose at bedtime is necessary to clarify the issue.

You may notice that your child shows basic improvement on the medication but now talks constantly, or breaks into tears, or explodes at the slightest frustration. Emotional instability does show up in some children who are taking psychostimulants, and we do not know how much of this results from the medication and how much stems from emotional problems. The medication does reduce muscle activity. This makes the child better able to interact and communicate, and a child who has quieted down may become more verbal. It is also possible that because the medication makes it possible for the child to sit still and become available for learning, the child is now forced to deal with the learning problems that were easy to avoid before. Frustration and anxiety mount, and this may explain excessive talking or other signs of emotional instability. If reassuring the child and assistance from the special-education team do not help to lessen these symptoms, you might ask your physician to decrease the drug dosage. If this does not help, you may have to consider stopping the medication.

The medication makes some children and adolescents tired or sleepy. They may walk around in a daze almost, or show little if any emotion. These behaviors suggest that the child is on too much medication. The calming effect is too great. Lowering the dose should correct the problems.

Some children or adolescents who do well on a psychostimulant may suddenly do worse when taking cold medicines that include an antihistamine. The sedative effect of the antihistamine appears to neutralize some of the stimulative effects of the psychostimulant. If this happens, your child may need an increased dosage of the psychostimulant while taking antihistamines.

Other Medications

No other group of medications works on Hyperactivity and Distractibility as successfully as the psychostimulants. Megavitamins, trace elements, and the elimination of specific food additives have been proposed as treatments for hyperactivity, and I discuss these approaches to treatment in Chapter 14. Here let us examine some other types of medication and their probable effects, just in case you hear of their use or in case they are suggested for your child.

The Major Tranquilizers

This group of drugs is used with people who have psychotic thinking disorders such as schizophrenia. The drugs in this category most frequently used are Thorazine, Mellaril, and Stelazine. They do nothing to decrease the Hyperactivity or the Distractibility of the learning disabled child or adolescent.

The Minor Tranquilizers

This group of drugs is more freely used in the general population to decrease anxiety. The most common ones are Librium, Valium, Miltown (or Equanil), Atarax, and Vistaril. None of these drugs has any effect on Hyperactivity or Distractibility although their use might decrease overactive behavior that is caused by anxiety.

The Antidepressants

We have noted that the psychostimulants are antidepressants. Another drug, Tofranil (generic name: imipramine), might work with Hyperactivity or Distractibility (see below).

The monoamine inhibitors, another type of antidepressant, do not help the conditions we are talking about.

Lithium, which is used successfully to stabilize mood swings with bipolar (manic-depressive) disorders, has not been found to help these conditions, either.

Seizure Medications

Dilantin and the other medications used for seizure disorders do not help to combat Hyperactivity or Distractibility.

Drugs for Specific Problems

Certain drugs may be prescribed by your physician for special behaviors. Haldol (generic name: haloperidol) may control involuntary spasms of one muscle or group of muscles, called "tics." Tofranil (generic name: imipramine) at bedtime may be used for bedwetting (enuresis). Incidentally, Tofranil affects the same brain chemicals as the psychostimulants, so if your child is on this medication, he or she may need a lighter dosage of the psychostimulant. Mellaril (generic name: thioridazine) at bedtime can minimize excessive nightmares temporarily. Valium (generic name: diazepam) can give temporary relief from night terrors, a state where the child appears to be awake but is still asleep while acting out a nightmare.

Getting Your Child's Cooperation

If your child or adolescent understands what the medicine does and how it works, he or she is more likely to cooperate. If the medication helps, the child will realize it and like being on it. Once this positive attitude is established, give your son or daughter some control over his or her own body by letting the youngster participate in decisions about what dosage is needed for different parts of the day. But if the child experiences no clear benefits, and teachers and family members don't see any improvement, he or she should not take it.

If you meet with resistance, discuss it fully with your son or daughter. Perhaps the child doesn't understand what the medication does. Maybe he or she sees it as a "bad pill"—every time the youngster misbehaves, mother or father says "Have you taken your pill today?" Maybe the child doesn't want the other kids to know about the pills. If that is the case, you will have to work out a plan for keeping it private.

Adolescents, especially, hate to be different. It is not unusual for someone who cooperated as a child to rebel against a regimen of medication as a teenager. Discuss this with your daughter or son and try to explain why the medicine is still important.

If, after all of your efforts, resistance persists, discuss it with your family doctor or with a mental health professional and come up with a plan of attack.

13

Treatment for Emotional, Social, and Family Problems

As I have said repeatedly, one critical question is whether emotional, social, or family problems are *causing* the academic difficulty or whether these problems are a *consequence* of the frustrations and failures brought on by academic difficulty. If the problems are a consequence of the learning disabilities, the initial focus should be on developing appropriate educational programs, starting any medication indicated, and educating or reeducating the family. After these stresses are alleviated, if the emotional, social, or family problems persist, you may need to look for clinical help.

We looked at some common problems of this type in earlier chapters. I have also discussed the evaluation process. Now let us look first at the different types of mental health professionals and psychological therapies that are commonly available. Then I shall discuss some behavior modification techniques that you can use at home to make family life smoother, whether or not your learning disabled youngster is in treatment.

The Mental Health Professionals

There are four kinds of mental health professionals: psychiatrists, psychologists, social workers, and psychiatric nurses. Each has a core of common knowledge and skills in diagnosis and treatment, as well as unique areas of expertise. Being an intelligent consumer requires that you learn all you can about the qualifications of any clinician who is going to work with your child or with your family. Don't be any less concerned about seeking the best qualified person in this field than you would be about selecting a brain surgeon.

Any of these professionals might practice one of several forms of therapy. Let me describe each kind of mental health professional first, then discuss the approaches to therapy.

The *psychiatrist* is, first of all, a medical doctor, a physician. A general psychiatrist has taken four to five years of additional specialized training after graduating from medical school. Part of this training includes experience in psychiatric work with children and adolescents. A child psychiatrist has completed the medical education and training to become a general psychiatrist and has then taken two additional years of training in child psychiatry. Because of her or his medical training, the general or child psychiatrist may be best able to differentiate the biological, psychological, and so-cial—the "bio-psychological"—aspects of a problem in order to establish a diagnosis. By law, only psychiatrists can prescribe med-ication or, in most states, admit patients to a psychiatric hospital. All psychiatrists are trained to do individual psychotherapy; most are also trained to do group, behavioral, and family therapy. The child psychiatrist, because of his or her additional training, specializes in the bio-psychosocial diagnosis and treatment of children and adolescents.

The *psychologist* may have a doctorate or master's degree. Some practice with a bachelor's degree, but most states do not license people with only this length of training. The advanced training may be in the clinical area, in counseling, or in school psychology. And there are other areas of specialization. The doctorate-level psychologist has completed four to six years of graduate training beyond college, including a year of special clinical training, or internship. Because one can be trained in so many areas and because so many different types of internships are available, any given psychologist probably has differing skills with different types of therapy. The depth and variety of training with children or adolescents also varies greatly. The master's level psychologist has completed a one- or two-year graduate program beyond college. Because training and experience vary so widely, you may want to discuss the background of your psychologist before starting any therapy. Note, however, that most psychologists do have the unique skill of being able to administer psychological testing.

The *social worker* has completed college plus two years in a graduate school of social work. Following this training, he or she usually works under supervision in a special agency or some other setting for several more years. Those who focus their work in the mental health field are often called "psychiatric social workers." The level of diagnostic and treatment skills when working with children and adolescents depends on the social worker's additional experience following graduation. So will the kinds of treatments and therapies offered. In certain settings, social workers with only bachelor's degrees may provide some services.

The *psychiatric nurse* may have completed a two-, three-, or four-year training program plus work experience in a psychiatric setting. To be certified as a Clinical Specialist, she or he must have a master's or doctor's degree in psychiatric or mental health nursing or an acceptable equivalent and must pass a national examination. The psychiatric nurse with graduate school training has core knowledge and skills comparable to those of the other mental health professionals with a similar level of training. Many focus on family therapy, but many are skilled in individual, behavioral, or group therapy with children and adolescents.

You can see that there are several professions within the mental health field, and within each profession, practitioners have widely different levels of training and experience. Not all are equally well-trained to work with children or adolescents. Be an intelligent, informed consumer. It is not inappropriate to discuss a person's training, experience, and specialty. After all, you are entrusting your child, and possibly your family to her or him. Be assertive. It is not rude to reject a therapist and look for another if you don't like the person or feel that he or she doesn't relate well to your child.

The Psychological Therapies

The various behaviors of children and adolescents reflect many kinds of emotional problems. Any evaluation looks at all aspects of behavior, and, depending on the findings, the evaluator(s) will recommend a type of therapy that best addresses the problems identified. Often, several problem areas are noted which call for a combination of treatments. The kinds of evaluations and the therapies they lead to include:

The *dynamic evaluation*, sometimes called the "psychoanalytic" or "intrapsychic" evaluation, can be done by talking with the child or, with a younger child, by interacting through play techniques. The evaluator looks at the interactions between internal thinking processes (basic wishes and needs, conscience or value systems), the ability to mediate what to do, and the realities of the outside world. He or she explores questions related to the relative strengths of each process, the coping mechanisms available to the child, the types of problems or conflicts the child is struggling with, and whether all of these factors are age-appropriate or not. If conflicts are found, *individual psychotherapy* might be recommended.

In a *behavioral evaluation*, the clinician observes and records behavior in an attempt to observe how the behaviors were learned and why they persist. If they are not successful or are dysfunctional, how might they be changed? What reinforces the behavior in the child or adolescent? Various types of *behavioral therapy* might be recommended.

The *interpersonal evaluation* often involves directly observing the child or adolescent in several settings or obtaining information from people who observe him or her in these settings. How does the child interact with peers and adults? What roles does he or she play? Are there patterns of behavior that explain difficulties in relating or communicating? If problems appear in these areas, *group therapy* might be recommended.

The *systems evaluation*, or family evaluation, looks at the most important system, the family. The family is seen together. What role does the child or adolescent play? What effect does this role have on other family members? What effect do the other family members have on the child? Difficulties in these areas might lead to *family therapy*.

By the time some children are evaluated, their problems have become so complex that a multiple approach is needed. The full family may be seen initially both to educate and to help parents regain control and confidence. At this time a behavior modification system might be introduced to assist in setting some limits on the child's or adolescent's unacceptable behaviors. Once the behavior is under control, the child or adolescent might be seen individually and the parents seen as a couple. The family continues to be seen together on occasion as well.

You can help your child or adolescent and your family in many ways. The first thing to do is to select a competent clinician, one who is well-trained, experienced, and skilled, and one you like and whom you feel you can talk to easily. Preferably, the clinician should be comfortable with more than one model of therapy and be flexible in using whichever approach is most helpful at any given time. The clinician must be knowledgeable about learning disabilities and the special problems of the learning disabled person and his or her family.

Preventive Family Counseling

When a full evaluation has been done, everyone in the family must hear and understand the results. I find it helpful to use from three to five one-hour sessions focused on preventive counseling to facilitate this process.

I meet with the parents initially to review all aspects of the evaluation. They must understand just what the learning disabilities are and grasp what types of special educational programs are needed. They must also understand how their child's learning disabilities relate to activities at home, in the neighborhood, and in sports and other activities. I introduce the concept of building on strengths rather than magnifying weaknesses. If medication is needed, I explain what it is and how the parents will work with me in managing it. I then go over the ways in which the child's disabilities may explain the emotional, social, and family problems. Before these initial sessions end, I might offer material to read or direct the parents to the people in school they must work with if they do not already know them.

Once the parents have begun to understand, I meet with the child and review all of the issues that I shared with the parents. The only difference is the way in which I communicate with a younger child, an older child, or an adolescent. I go over each test and explain the results. For most, this session is the most important one ever held. For the first time these children understand why they are the way they are and why they have problems. They realize that they are not bad or stupid or lazy. I end by reviewing the full treatment plan, including plans for school and home. If medication or other therapies are needed, I discuss them too.

Once the child or adolescent begins to understand, I schedule a family session. We review the full evaluation again. Every member of the family needs to know and understand the problems and the treatment plans. The brothers and sisters need to have a chance to ask questions and share their concerns. With understanding, the child's image and role in the family begins to shift. Siblings may become allies in the battle to help.

With this preventive counseling approach to the total child and family, many, if not most, of the children and their families relax and make progress. Social, emotional, and family problems diminish as stresses are relieved and opportunities for positive relationships and successes are increased. Those who improve too slowly or not at all may need some type of psychological therapy. Recommendations for such therapy are often best delayed until the effects of counseling can be observed.

There must be follow-up support in working with the school, and you may have to try different strategies. Often I meet with a family once or twice a year to assess progress and think through the next steps, sometimes on a long-term basis. Some of the children of families who started with me when they were in early elementary school are now in high school, working, or in college.

I believe that the major goal of any intervention with a family is to educate them so that they can become informed consumers and assertive advocates. As the child begins to grow up, gradually she or he takes on this role. Eventually that person must accept responsibility for planning and living his or her own life.

Sometimes some of the child's learning disabilities remain in the adult. The adolescent or young adult must know about this in order to plan intelligently. I recently received a call from a young woman I had worked with since she was in the third grade. Now in the first year of dental school, she was home on her winter break. She started by saying, "It never ends." I asked what was happening. She explained that she had just had her first experience in the dental clinic using instruments. "I tried to examine someone's teeth using the dental mirror and got all mixed up. . . . All those years of teaching myself left to right, left to right and now it's all backwards again. . . . My brain was so confused." I started to say that I knew someone in her town who could help. She stopped me and said, "Don't worry, I'll figure it out . . . I just called to say hello."

Managing Unacceptable Behavior at Home

Whether or not your child or adolescent receives professional therapy, certain measures that you can try at home will help you and your family to manage and control your child's unacceptable behavior better. If you run into difficulty, your son's or daughter's behaviors may be too internalized to change without special help, or other family problems may be interfering. It can't hurt to try, however.

The child's pain and frustration may have spread to the entire family. Tantrums and negativism may have erupted in power battles that no one wins. I meet parents who describe their child as a tyrant who must have his or her way or all hell breaks loose—screaming, throwing things, hitting sisters or brothers, messing up his or her room, or "something." Later I meet a 4-foot, 70-pound little boy who can be picked up and carried under one arm. Where *is* this monster?

When I start working with the family, I soon find out. The child's behavior *does* dominate the family. The parents avoid confrontations because they don't want to face the consequences. They "look the other way" until pushed so far that they have to react. By that time, the only possible reaction is anger. They yell, hit the child, or give out a punishment—"No TV for a week!"—then have to back down because they have no way to enforce it.

Without meaning to do so, many parents reinforce the very behavior they do not want. The child acts naughty and gets a lot of attention, negative attention. The parents get upset and this proves to the child that she or he *can* control one part of the world, the family. This, along with getting what the child wants, is the reward for bad behavior. Your other children see you forced to give in. They remind you that their brother or sister gets away with murder. Worse, when the child is good you are so relieved that you may not react at all. Soon the child learns the lesson that the only way to get attention is to be bad.

How do you reverse this pattern? How do you regain control? How can you change this behavior—for your sake, the family's sake, and, most important, for your child's sake? Such negative control of parents is unhealthy and unproductive for the child. He or she must learn different behavior patterns before trying out similar manipulations in school and in society.

One approach involves *behavior management*. You define the behaviors you want to change, then develop a systematic approach to making those changes. This helps you to understand better how your behavior interacts with your son's or daughter's. When the plan works, you regain control, feel less angry, and begin to enjoy, rather than dread, interacting with your child.

Identifying the Behaviors

First, list the specific behaviors that concern you. You may try this on your own, or a mental health clinician may help you. If you are two parents, both of you should make up the list together. One model to use is an "A-B-C" approach. Each day, each parent fills in a chart that includes the following categories: *A*, which stands for "antecedent," that is, what happened before the unacceptable behavior; *B*, which stands for the "behavior" you observed; and *C*, which stands for the "consequences," what happened because of the behavior. For example:

Date/Time	Antecedent	Behavior	Consequence
Monday 4:30 PM	Don't know; not there	John hit sister; she hit back	Told both to go to room
6:00 PM	Talking to Mary	John teased her; she cried	Yelled at John
9:00 PM	Told John to get ready for bed.	Refused to take bath, get in PJs; yelled at me when told.	Took 30 min. of reminding; finally hit him and he went to take bath

Certain patterns should become clear after a week of keeping these records. For example, the consequences that follow the same behavior may be inconsistent; or you get mad and yell at everything; or other family members get punished as much as the son or daughter who causes the problems. You may find a pattern of antecedents and behaviors. When John doesn't get his way, doesn't like what he has to do, or sees someone getting your attention, he acts up.

Don't be surprised if one parent's list differs from the other one's. When there are two parents, one often is the firm disciplinarian and the other, the easy-going, "give-them-another-chance" type. Each parent sees and lists different things. Furthermore, each of you has different experiences and expectations. Father may come home at 6:00 or 6:30 in the evening looking forward to being with, and maybe playing with, the kids. Frustrated and short of temper, mother has had it by then and wants the kids to be quiet and get their homework and their other chores done so that they can get to bed. Neither parent is right or wrong, nor is there just one way to bring up children. The important goal is that both parents agree on their expectations and be consistent in asking that they be met.

Study your chart and make a list of the behaviors that you find unacceptable, that cause difficulties in the family. Then see if you can understand each other's lists and see if you can agree on a common list. If you can't, this might be the first clue to a problem, and you might need outside professional help to proceed.

Frequently, the objectionable behaviors fall into three groups:

Physical abuse

* hits siblings
  hits parent
  hurts pet
  or_____

Verbal abuse

* yells at siblings
* yells at parent
* teases siblings
  curses
  or_____

Noncompliance

* Won't listen to what you say
  Doesn't follow family rules
  Doesn't do required chores
  Defies your requests
  or_____

Setting Up a Program

Once you have a clear idea of the behaviors that you want to change, you need to define the behavior clearly and to work out a consequence that you can impose consistently. Work out your new plan in detail, then introduce it to your family. Ideally, all of your children should participate in the program. Even if your other sons and daughters do not cause problems, it will not affect them negatively, and it may actually benefit them by rewarding their good behavior.

There are many approaches to changing behavior, and many good books are available on the subject, *Parent Effectiveness Training*, by Dr. Thomas Gordon (Wyden Publishers), for one. If you seek help, your clinician may come up with a better approach for your specific family than those I discuss here. The final plan must be one you are comfortable with, one that you can act on every time, and one that fits with your beliefs about child-rearing.

In general, you want to reverse the pattern of punishing bad behavior and usually ignoring or only occasionally rewarding good or positive behavior. Your new plan should reward positive behavior and withhold rewards for negative behavior. And you should come up with preplanned responses that you can use every time so that your son or daughter cannot catch you off guard, making you feel helpless and therefore angry.

First, divide the typical school day into three parts: (1) from the time your daughter or son gets up until she or he leaves for school; (2) from the time she or he returns from school until the end of the evening meal; and (3) from the end of this meal until the child goes to sleep. Try to develop a similar three-unit breakdown for weekend or summer days.

Now make a list of your child's unacceptable behaviors. Your first list should be brief and limited to the major problems. For example,

1. No physical abuse (define in detail: hitting sister, pulling the cat's tail, kicking mother in the shins).

2. No verbal abuse (again, define in detail: no cursing, or calling someone "stupid").

3. No compliance, that is refusing to do what the child is told to do. Make it clear that you will make a request once and repeat it a second time. Following this, you will warn *only once more*. If the child does not comply on the next request, that will be considered noncompliance. You still expect the child to do what you asked, but he or she has also acted unacceptably and is subject to the consequences you have established.

Your purpose is to reward positive behavior. Negative behavior results either in loss of "earning points" or in "time out"—that is, the child will be removed from the family for a limited time.

Let's start with the *earning points*. Your child or adolescent can earn 1 point for each negative behavior *not* acted out. For example, your son knows that he is not supposed to abuse anyone and is supposed to do his chores. As he leaves for school, you might say, "You called your sister stupid, but I'm pleased that you didn't hit anyone and you did put your dishes in the sink when I asked you to. So you earn 2 of your 3 points." You might say to your daughter, "You did everything right this morning, and I'm delighted. Thank you for not yelling back when your brother teased you. You get all 3 points." Have a book or chart available and record the points. In the past, you might have scolded your son, rewarding him by giving him your attention, while ignoring your daughter. This plan allows you to pay attention to everybody.

Handle each part of the day in the same way. The maximum points earned can be 9 a day, or 63 a week. These points can be used in three ways—for a daily reward, a weekly reward, and a special reward. Your children can check the book to see how many points they have.

Each reward must be individualized for each member of the family, and each must be compatible with your family's habits and philosophy. The *daily reward* could be an additional half hour of TV if your family limits TV, or being able to stay up thirty minutes past the child's usual bedtime, or having fifteen or thirty minutes of special time alone with a parent for a favorite activity—anything that is self-limited and possible to do. The *weekly reward* might be going to a movie or a favorite fast-food restaurant, having a friend sleep over, or anything else that is special and not usually expected. Some families use money: Each point is worth a penny, let's say, or 5 or 10 cents, depending on the child's age.

For the daily and weekly rewards, set a goal of 80 percent of the maximum points. One needs 7 points for the daily reward and 50 points for the weekly reward. After three or four weeks, raise the goal you expect to 90 percent (8 points daily, 57 weekly). It is best not to set 100 percent as a goal. Any negative behavior early in the day or week then destroys all hopes of a reward, so the child may just give up.

Work out these rewards with your children. Let them participate in selecting the rewards that seem most meaningful to them. This is also true for the *special reward*. Try to pick something both special and realistic—a trip to an amusement park, a new bike, a special record, a stereo or radio. Don't go overboard, but make it worth working toward. Select a reasonable number of points as a goal, making sure that it takes at least three to five weeks to reach that number. For example, as soon as the child earns 225 points, you will contribute half the cost of a new bike. Your daughter or son will have to save up or earn the other half of the price or wait for the next time they earn 225 points to receive the other half.

Remember, this plan is for everyone. Negotiate with each child or adolescent. It wouldn't be fair unless all of them are rewarded for their positive behavior.

Now for the concept of *time out*. Before you start, define those behaviors that are so unacceptable—hitting people, or cursing, for example—that they will result in the child's being removed from the family for a limited time. Keep the list brief. Such behaviors not only result in losing a point for that unit of time, they also mean removal from the family for fifteen minutes. This time is to be spent quietly, thinking about what happened and why she or he was sent off alone. You can send the child to his or her room if you can remove the TV, radio, stereo, games, or other pleasurable distractions. Or you can use the laundry room, a spare room, or some place else that is easy to isolate and that provides no opportunity to have fun. The door is to be closed, and the child is to be quiet. Each time the child opens the door, yells, or throws things around the room, the time is reset to zero, and the fifteen minutes start over. Some parents use a kitchen timer that can be set and reset and that sounds a bell when the time is up. If you think that your son or daughter will refuse to go into the room and stay there, you might seek the help of a mental health professional to work out another initial approach.

You can use time outs away from home as well. If you are in a restaurant, use the car. If you are shopping, find a place for the child to sit and tell her or him that you will return in fifteen minutes.

This *earning points/time out* system must be planned in advance, ideally by the whole family. If the child or adolescent you are concerned about refuses to participate, sit down with everyone else and make your plans. Tell the child that he or she is welcome to join in, but that it's OK to refuse—the rest of the family will simply plan for him or her.

For the plan to work, you must be exact as to expectations, behaviors, rewards, and consequences. You must be fair, keep good records, and be consistent. It may be rough in the beginning. The child will find every loophole in the system. But if you stick with the plan and make all the revisions necessary, you will see change. Rewarding behaviors you want rather than punishing behaviors you do not want does work.

Additional Plans

As you go along, you can add to this basic system. *Learning discussions*, for example, are conversations between you and the child or adolescent having the difficulty. Initially they are best held after the fact. There has been a blow-up, or a fight, or a yelling match, and you have sent your son to his room. Later in the day, or before bed time, sit down with the boy in a quiet place when no one else is around and discuss what happened privately. "Fred, I'm sorry you had so much trouble this afternoon. I love you and I don't like being angry with your behavior or having to remove you from the family. What do you think we can do to stop such things from happening?" Let him talk. At first you may hear only angry accusations of "unfairness." Fred blames everyone but himself. Try to understand how the boy saw and experienced things, and suggest alternative behaviors. "I don't know if your brother was teasing you before you hit him or not. I wasn't there. But let's suppose he did. What else could you have done? By hitting him you got into trouble and he didn't. There must be a better way. Maybe you could have told me what you thought he was doing?" If you two agree on a strategy, be sure to follow through. Your son or daughter may be too angry, at first, to understand what you're saying. But you will have started a way of thinking and shared problem-solving. Soon the child will join in.

Once this approach is in place, whenever possible try to have your learning discussions before the fact. "Fred, you and I both know that if you keep playing with your brother, once the teasing starts there will be a fight. Do you remember what we talked about? What else could you do?" Or, "Alice, you're forcing me to be a policeman and to yell at you or punish you. I don't like doing that. I'd rather enjoy being with you than yelling at you or punishing you. Why do you force me to be a policeman? Remember what we talked about the other night?"

You may be surprised at how your child opens up and becomes available to talking about his or her behavior. He or she can also learn from hearing you openly discuss your feelings and thoughts.

Let the child see how you feel—angry, sad, afraid, worried—and how you handle these feelings. If you feel angry, say so. "I'm so angry right now at what you did that I can't talk to you. I'm going in the other room to calm down. Later, we can talk." Not only will you help yourself, you will be giving your child a model for handling anger.

Having an acceptable model for expressing feelings is important. Many families are quick to tell their children how they may *not* show anger or sadness, but they don't teach them acceptable ways of showing these feelings. Anger is a normal feeling, and children must learn how to handle it acceptably. This will vary from family to family. Can the children yell as long as they don't curse? Can they stamp their feet as long as they don't break things? Watch out for confusing messages. When father gets angry, he yells or throws things. But when your child gets angry and imitates father's behavior, you get upset.

Let's be honest: Most families have different rules for adults than for children. Be that as it may, you still owe it to your children to help them learn acceptable ways to express their feelings in ways appropriate to their positions in your family.

Handling Chores

You may need to clarify what is expected from each family member. In many families, everyone assumes that they must help and no one needs to be told. If your family is not this way, if people do not do their share of family work, or if you have to remind them constantly, you should work on this problem.

Make a list of all individual and family chores. Individual ones might be putting dirty clothes in the hamper, making one's bed, picking things up off the floor of the bedroom, and so on. Family chores might be setting the table, clearing the table, loading or emptying the dishwasher, vacuuming, and so forth. Put up the list of individual chores in an obvious place, on the refrigerator or a bulletin board in the kitchen, say, with clear instructions. These chores are not necessarily rewarded, they are *expected*. If they are not done, you must establish consistent consequences. You can negotiate this with the kids, but *you* make the final decisions. Be exact—Adriana's bed must be made before she leaves for school; Aaron must set the table before 6:00 P.M.

Family chores are shared. Fights usually start when one child feels that she or he has more work to do that the other children.

Work out a specific plan, set up a calendar, and post it for all to see. For example:

Setting the table; putting dishes away	Mary: even-numbered days Billy: odd-numbered days
Clearing the table; washing dishes	Mary: odd-numbered days Billy: even-numbered days
Vacuum all first-floor rooms	Mary:1st, 3rd, 5th week Billy: 2nd, 4th week
Empty clothes dryer and put clothes in each person's room	Mary: 2nd and 4th week Billy: 1st, 3rd, 5th week

The consequences of not doing these chores must fit your family style. Here are two possible ways to establish them. You might come up with others, or a professional might help you to work this out.

The "Maid Service"

Establish the parent services that are not supplied free of charge. If chores are not done by the set time, you will do them, but not for free. Set a fee, say 25 cents per bed, or 50 cents for picking up the room. Don't argue or remind. If the chore is not done on time, do it for the child and submit a bill. Collect the money from the child's allowance or withdraw it from her or his birthday or savings money. If the child has no money, work out a plan for earning money. This works for many children and adolescents. One bill, and they think twice about "forgetting."

The "Sunday Box"

Set up a box in a secure place, a closet or room that can be locked, for example. Make it clear that any items left where they should not be—toys, bikes, books, papers, baseballs, clothes, coats, shoes—after a predetermined time of the day will be placed in the box (or closet) which will be emptied on Sunday morning. This means that if a child's favorite game, or bike, is left lying out, it is lost to them until Sunday. This model doesn't work for clothes that are needed daily, and you may get around this by charging a fee to retrieve such items before Sunday. One mother found this system so successful that she put her husband on the plan, and it worked for him, too.

You should set up chores that your children can do to earn extra money—cutting the grass, washing clothes, washing the kitchen floor, cleaning the garage, for instance. If your son or daughter owes you money for maid service or for anything else, assign such chores so that they can earn enough money to pay you. (This is also a way for them to earn extra money for themselves.)

Handling Property Damage

How should you handle behavior that results in property damage—broken furniture, doors, walls, other people's property? Your son throws a glass and breaks it. Your daughter gets mad and breaks another child's toy. First, depending on your family plan, the child might lose points or spend time in his or her room. But this isn't enough to stop the behavior: The child should pay to repair or replace the item. Money can come out of an allowance (installments each week if they owe a lot) or a savings account, or the child can work on the chores you have set up that earn money. The first time your daughter gets angry, kicks over a lamp and breaks it, then learns that it will cost her $50, she will think twice about such behavior in the future. And this is our goal—getting the child to think before he or she acts, to think about the consequences of each behavior, then to select the behavior that is most acceptable and least painful.

Further, brothers and sisters who have had to live with broken or torn things now find that their things are replaced. They will be much more willing to cooperate with your plan than fighting back or getting even when they see that you follow through with consequences.

Handling Dawdling

What can you do if your child daydreams or just plays around when he or she is supposed to be getting dressed or undressed or finishing a task—that is, when he or she dawdles? First, don't get yourself in a position where you have to remind, nag, yell, scream, and then, in anger, do the task for the child. All this does is teach the child that he or she can get away with it or can succeed in getting you upset. Next, you must have set a clearly defined and consistently enforced consequences. The following examples should suggest something that fits your child and your family.

Your young daughter never gets dressed on time. As the time for the school bus gets closer and she has not yet eaten, you go into her bedroom, storm at her, then quickly dress her so that she can eat and leave for school on time. You are upset and angry, and she has succeeded both in getting you upset and in getting you to dress her.

You might work out the following plan with your school staff and the bus driver. Let's say the bus arrives at 7:55 A.M. Announce that breakfast will be served from 7:15 to 7:45 A.M. only, and it will be provided only to the child who is dressed. At 7:50, quietly take all the clothes she has not yet put on and place them in a bag, wrap your daughter in a robe or coat, and walk her to the bus, pajamas and all. The bus driver, having been briefed, smiles and says hello. If she arrives at school still not dressed, her teacher quietly tells her to go to the bathroom or the cloakroom and get dressed, then come to class. She won't starve without breakfast, but she will be shocked and embarrassed. She will also change her behavior and relieve you of your role as policeman and dresser.

This approach also works in other situations. At bedtime, whether in pajamas or still in street clothes, put the child to bed and turn out the lights. When the family is leaving for a movie, or a visit, or a shopping trip, and the child is not ready by the appointed time, you leave with the rest of the family. If your child cannot be left alone, have a sitter on call so that you can follow through with your plan. Once you call the sitter, it is too late to change plans. Once again, after a time or two of losing out on the family fun rather than controlling the family and spoiling everyone else's fun, the child will get the message: "Finish your tasks on time or accept the consequences. You lose, not the rest of us."

In Summary

One of the important goals of psychotherapy is to encourage the patient to change unacceptable behavior patterns and to try new, more fulfilling ones which succeed better at less cost. Your child may well be receiving some kind of individual therapy—and you may be in family therapy—working toward just such ends.

Working at home to encourage desirable behaviors from the child rather than punishing or inadvertently reinforcing objectionable behaviors in no way interferes with any other treatment. If you are unsure, check with the mental health professional your child is seeing and get her or his reassurance and help and advice.

The approaches I have outlined here—or your own variations of them—will work, however, only if you construct your plan in advance, educate the whole family in what the plan is and what it is supposed to do, and consistently *follow through* on it. The technique involves hard work, but it is guaranteed to result in a happier, better functioning family.

14

The Controversial Therapies

We do not know very much about many aspects of the learning disabilities, Hyperactivity, and Distractibility. I have outlined the several acceptable approaches to treatment. Less acceptable, more controversial approaches to treatment also exist. The controversy over some of these treatments relates to the basic theory behind the treatment; over others, it relates to how the treatment is used.

The acceptable treatment plans take a long time and a lot of work. Training children—and parents—to compensate for problems while retraining them in better learning and coping skills is a slow, laborious process. I can understand that you would want to try almost any approach that might work better and faster. But you must be an intelligent consumer. Before committing yourself and especially your daughter or son to any new or different approach, ask questions. Your physician or one of the organizations listed in the Appendix can provide you with more information.

Neurophysiological Approaches

These neurophysiological approaches take as their basic premise the notion that some area of nervous system activity is not functioning properly. They hold that by stimulating certain impulses to the brain, by exercising specific muscle patterns, or by chemically correcting the dysfunctional system, brain function will be improved.

Patterning

You probably know of some family that has their child on a routine of crawling and other exercises. These routines must be practiced regularly, and a group of neighbors may have volunteered to help. Possibly, you have thought about this approach for your son or daughter. Patterning has been suggested as a treatment for learning disabilities.

The theory and techniques of "patterning" were initially developed by Robert Doman and Carl Delacato. They proposed that failure to pass properly through a certain sequence of developmental stages in movement, language, and competence in the manual, visual, auditory, and tactile areas reflected poor neurological organization, and that poor organization may indicate brain damage. As described by Doman and Delacato, patterning reaches "the brain itself by pouring into the afferent sensory system . . . all of the stimuli normally provided by (the child's) environment but with such intensity and frequency as to draw, ultimately, a response from the corresponding motor systems." In more severe cases of brain damage, passive movement patterns are imposed with the goal of producing the normal activities that the injured brain area would have produced had it not been damaged.

In addition to those methods of manipulation, other patterning techniques include sensory stimulation; rebreathing of exhaled air using a plastic face mask, alleged to increase breathing capacity and to stimulate blood flow to the brain; and restriction of fluid, salt, and sugar intake, alleged to decrease the production of brain fluid (cerebrospinal fluid) and brain irritability.

The American Academy of Pediatrics, the American Academy of Cerebral Palsy, the United Cerebral Palsy Association of Texas, and the Canadian Association for Retarded Children have published statements expressing concern about the effectiveness of this form of therapy. My own opinion is that the patterning approaches do nothing to help learning disabilities, Hyperactivity, or Distractibility.

Optometric Training

Opinions about optometric training differ in part over basic theory and in part over treatment applications.

Ophthalmologists, that is, physicians specializing in eye diseases, believe that when a child or adolescent with learning disabilities is referred to them they should check for problems with vision—nearsightedness, farsightedness, astigmatism and so on—and with eye-muscle imbalance, and for any ocular disease. If they find any of these problems, they prescribe treatment. If they do not find any of these problems, they believe that the child should be referred to a special educator or some other appropriate specialist for treatment of his or her learning disabilities.

Optometrists have doctor's degrees from professional schools of optometry, but they are not physicians. They look for the same problems that ophthalmologists do. But after they have ruled out problems or treated the problems they find, many optometrists believe they can also treat the learning disabilities.

Most optometrists evaluate the child's visual abilities and may prescribe glasses or the use of visual training or eye-muscle training techniques if these are indicated. Another group of optometrists use a developmental vision approach and see a broader role for the optometrist in learning problems. They feel that learning in general, and reading in particular, require high levels of visual perception. They point out that visual perception processes are also related to the child's sensory-motor coordination. To correct visual perceptual problems, they employ a wide variety of educational and sensory-motor-perceptual training techniques in an attempt to correct educational problems in children. It is this subgroup of optometrists who have been active with children with learning disabilities.

The American Academy of Pediatrics, the American Academy of Ophthalmology and Otolaryngology, and the American Association of Ophthalmology issued a joint statement which criticizes this approach. This joint communique emphasizes the need for a multidisciplinary approach to learning disabilities. No one professional can evaluate and treat the whole child. The statement further cautions that there are no peripheral eye defects that can produce dyslexia and associated learning disabilities. It minimizes the effect of visual or neurological organization training as optometrists use it. It states that glasses have no value in treating learning problems except where there is a visual problem. And it concludes that the treatment of learning disabilities is primarily for the special educator. The full position of the American Academy of Ophthalmology can be obtained by writing to the Academy (the address is listed in the Appendix).

This controversy between ophthalmologists and optometrists is just one of many confusing disagreements that catch the parents in the middle as they try to decide what is best for their child.

You will undoubtedly hear views and counterviews from those on both sides of the fence, and you must make up your own mind. My own concerns about optometrists who attempt to treat total learning disabilities stem from my treatment concepts. I believe that a team approach must be used to evaluate children with learning disabilities. If only an optometrist sees a child or an adolescent, that person may recognize visual perception or visual motor disabilities but may not test for auditory or language disabilities. I also feel that help should be provided in an educational setting and should be related to educational tasks.

Sensory Integration Therapy

Many occupational therapists approach certain types of learning disabilities by having the child or adolescent do exercises. But some therapists may try to stimulate the balance mechanisms of the body, called the "vestibular system," by certain exercises, using eardrops or chairs that spin. They may stimulate touch sensations, called "tactile sensations," by using cloths or brushes rubbed against the skin. This process is called "somatosensory stimulation." These last two approaches are based on the research of Dr. A. Jean Ayres.

Dr. Ayres's research suggests that the capacity of the brain to react to auditory and visual processes depends on the brain stem's ability to organize them. If the brain stem is inadequate to organize these sensory integrative processes, the person may have learning disabilities. Her research data suggest that some disorders are consistently observed in learning disabled children. These problems, which can be accounted for in terms of inadequate sensory integration in the brain stem, include: immature muscle control, poorly developed visual orientation to environmental space, difficulty in the processing of sound into percepts, and a tendency toward distractibility.

Ayres proposes that carefully controlled sensory input can be introduced through the vestibular and somatosensory systems. Graded stimulation like this, she believes, enhances the capacity of the brain for intersensory integration. This allows for improved interconnections between the vestibular and tactile senses and the visual and auditory inputs. The therapy models based on these concepts suggest that vestibular stimulation helps to rectify the auditory language disorders of learning disabled children.

I have the same concern with occupational therapists who practice this approach in isolation as I have with some optometrists. Once again, I believe that a *team* evaluation is necessary. An occupational therapist may diagnose a child's motor disabilities but not test for other areas of possible learning disability. As part of the team, the occupational therapist can play an important role in diagnosis and treatment efforts, but interventions are best related to educational tasks.

Cerebellar-Vestibular Dysfunction

In 1981, Dr. Harold Levinson published a book in which he suggested that some forms of dyslexia are caused by dysfunction in the nerve pathways and in interactions between the balance, or vestibular, system in the ear and the cerebellum, that part of the brain which coordinates balance. He proposes that this disability can be corrected by using medications such as those used for motion sickness. He reports that the dyslexia improves or disappears in patients on this medication.

I have read the book. Levinson cites his research, but most of it has not yet been published in scientific journals and other researchers have not yet been able to test out his results. At this time, then, there is no evidence on which to conclude that this approach is correct. The research to prove or disprove the theory and treatment has yet to be done.

Orthomolecular Approaches

Orthomolecular medicine is defined as the treatment of disorders by providing the optimum molecular environment for the mind, especially the optimum concentrations of substances normally present in the human body. Several orthomolecular treatment approaches have been suggested for the child with learning disabilities.

Megavitamins

The use of massive doses of vitamins to treat emotional and thinking disorders began with the treatment of schizophrenia. One researcher, Dr. Humphrey Osmond, suggested that schizophrenia was caused by an improper breakdown of certain chemicals normally found in the brain. Then Dr. Abram Hoffer and Dr. Osmond proposed that administration of large quantities of certain B vitamins could stop this faulty breakdown.

To date, no documented biochemical studies on schizophrenic patients have confirmed the theory that Hoffer and Osmond proposed. A five-year study carried out by the Board of Directors of the Canadian Mental Health Association strongly suggested that this treatment had no therapeutic effect. After reviewing the history and literature relating to this subject, the members of an American Psychiatric Association task force concluded in their report, "Megavitamins and Orthomolecular Therapy in Psychiatry," that there is no valid basis for the use of megavitamins in the treatment of mental disorders. The American Academy of Pediatrics has also reported no validity to this concept.

Dr. Allan Cott wrote the first paper suggesting megavitamin treatment for children with learning disabilities in 1971. His conclusion that megavitamins can help these children has not been confirmed by other researchers. Despite these negative results, the approach remains popular.

Trace Elements

Certain chemicals exist in our body in very small quantities, called "trace elements." These trace elements, including copper, zinc, manganese, magnesium, and chromium, along with more common elements such as calcium, potassium, sodium, and iron, are necessary nutrients—that is, their presence is essential for maintenance of normal physiological function.

In many parts of the United States, children are treated with trace-element replacement therapy, but we have no research to show that such treatment can correct learning disabilities.

Hypoglycemia

The term "hypoglycemia" refers to a clinical situation where the blood sugar level is below normal. Another orthomolecular approach to learning disabilities regards them as secondary to hypoglycemia. The treatment, then, is to place the child on a diet for hypoglycemics—six or more small meals a day with minimal carbohydrates in each. Yet we have no research, or evidence of any kind, that establishes hypoglycemia as a cause of learning disabilities.

I have seen children on hypoglycemic diets because their parents read about them, or because someone who was not a physician recommended them. Do not use this treatment unless a physician has done a glucose tolerance test to confirm that your son or daughter is truly hypoglycemic.

Allergic Reactions

Several researchers have suggested that some types of learning disabilities may result from an allergic sensitivity of the central nervous system to specific foods. They discuss specific test procedures for establishing this as a possible factor. The relationship between food allergies and learning disabilities is still undergoing research.

You may meet professionals who are convinced that food allergies cause learning disabilities and others who disagree. Until more research is done, you will have to use your best judgment in trying this approach.

Food Additives: Dyes, Flavors, and Preservatives

In 1975, Dr. Benjamin Feingold published a book called *Why Your Child is Hyperactive* in which he proposed that synthetic flavors and colors in the diet were related to hyperactivity. He and his book received wide publicity. Feingold reported that the elimination of foods containing artificial colors and flavors, as well as salicylates and certain other additives, stopped hyperactivity. He based this thesis on clinical experience. Hoping that Feingold might be correct but needing to prove or disprove his theory, several research groups began to study this problem. Basically, they did two different types of clinical studies. One used a dietary crossover technique, the other, a specific-challenge approach.

In the *diet crossover studies,* Hyperactive children were randomly assigned at first either to the additive elimination diet or to a control—that is, a normal—diet, then crossed over to the other diet. The finds were ambiguous. Behavior improvement was noted in a few children by their teachers, but only when the control diet was given first, and then the elimination diet. No improvement was noted when the order was reversed.

The researchers summarized their findings by concluding that there may be a subset of Hyperactive children, particularly younger Hyperactive children, who respond to some aspect of the elimination diet, but either such a group is very small or the effectiveness of the diet is much less dramatic and predictable than previous anecdotal reports had described.

The imprecision of the diet crossover studies showed the need for a different research approach. The strategy was changed from testing the general efficacy of the over-all elimination diet to considering the specific involvement of artificial colors or flavors with Hyperactive children. In this *specific-challenge design,* the children were maintained on Feingold's elimination diet throughout the study. Periodically, they were given—the phrase for this is "challenged with"—foods that contained a suspected offending chemical, artificial food colors, for example. The researchers then noted whether a Hyperactive state was precipitated or aggravated by this challenge. The group using this approach concluded:

1. There does appear to be a subset of children with behavioral disturbances (Hyperactivity) who respond to some aspects of Feingold's diet. However, the controlled clinical studies indicate that this group is either small or that response is much less dramatic or predictable than was originally hypothesized.

2. With notable exceptions, the specific elimination of synthetic food colors from the diet does not appear to be a major factor in the reported responses of a majority of these children.

What does all of this mean? The results of this five-year effort at several research centers suggest that many of the Hyperactive children studied improved because of the "placebo" effect of the diet. In other words, the interest and extra attention given to the children caused the improvements. A small group of children, possibly 3 to 5 percent, did become very irritable and hyperactive within minutes after being challenged with certain food additives. This behavior lasted twenty to thirty minutes.

I will say it again. You must be informed, intelligent, consumers. I do not recommend the diet, but I will not discourage any parent who wants to try it.

Part Five

Legal Issues

15

Legal Issues of Importance to Parents

Fortunately for your son or daughter, and for you, today there are laws that require school systems to provide services for children with learning disabilities. This was not always the case. Before 1975, about half of the handicapped children in this country could not get an appropriate education. About one million were excluded from the public school system entirely. For the child with learning disabilities the situation was worse—about 90 percent were not even identified.

These laws, however, do not automatically assure that your child or adolescent will receive the educational programs he or she needs. As I have noted repeatedly, you must be an *informed consumer* and an *assertive advocate*: You must know the laws and know your rights, and then you must work actively with the school while insisting on these rights. The school personnel care about the education of *all* students. You care especially about the education of *your* student.

What are these laws? What do they mean for your son or daughter? What must you know and do to assure the best help you can possibly get? What can you do if you are not happy with your school's effort? Let me try to address these questions.

Parent Power

The major force behind today's legislation was a consumer movement led by organizations of parents of handicapped children. Later, the handicapped people themselves joined in this effort. They focused on the lack of an appropriate public education and on the exclusion of children or adolescents from programs provided by the public education system.

In the 1960s various groups of parents whose children had different handicaps, used publicity, mass mailings, public meetings, and other well-organized opinion-molding techniques to put pressure on state legislatures. They wanted laws making educational opportunities for the handicapped not simply available but mandatory. Most states responded with legislation, some more than others. A few states did nothing. Most of the more progressive state governments passed the laws but provided no enabling funds for facilities or trained professionals to carry out their intent. The focus of these pressure groups then shifted toward enactment of a federal law that could have an impact on all states.

In 1971, the Pennsylvania Association for Retarded Citizens filed a suit in that state which directly involved the federal government in these issues for the first time. Citing constitutional guarantees of due process and equal protection under the law, they argued that the access of retarded children to public education should be equal to that afforded other children. The court agreed. A year later the Federal Court in the District of Columbia made a similar ruling involving not only the mentally retarded but those with a wide range of handicaps. This 1972 decision established two major precedents critical to future progress: (1) Handicapped children have the right to a "suitable publicly supported education, regardless of the degree of the child's mental, physical, or emotional disability or impairment; and (2), concerning financing, "if sufficient funds are not available to finance all of the services and programs that are needed and desirable . . . the available funds must be expended equitably in such a manner that no child is entirely excluded from a publicly supported education." Over forty such cases were won throughout the United States following these two landmark decisions.

These court actions also had a profound influence on federal legislation. The Rehabilitation Act of 1973, referred to as "The Civil Rights Act for the Handicapped," prohibits discrimination on the basis of physical or mental handicaps in every federally assisted program in the country. Public education, of course, accepts federal assistance. Section 504 of this law focuses on the rights of the individual people in these programs, and it has been the keystone of parents' demands and of numerous successful court actions. The most critical issues in this section are:

1. As disabled job applicants or employees, handicapped people have the same rights and must be guaranteed the same benefits as nonhandicapped applicants and employees.

2. They are entitled to all of the medical services and medically related instruction that is available to the general public.

3. They are entitled to participate in vocational rehabilitation, day care, or any other social service program receiving Federal assistance on an equal basis with the nonhandicapped.

4. They have the equal rights to go to college or to enroll in a job-training or adult post-high-school basic education programs. Selection must be based on academic or other school records, and the disability cannot be a factor. (If a person has learning disabilities, the standard entrance testing procedures, the Scholastic Aptitude Test, for example, can be modified, and admission standards can be based on potential as well as on past performance.)

5. State and local school districts must provide an appropriate elementary and secondary education for all handicapped students.

This last part of Section 504 became the basis for Public Law 94-142, the "Education for All Handicapped Children Act," which was passed overwhelmingly by the House and Senate and enacted in November of 1976. This landmark legislation capped an heroic effort begun by a few parents who joined with others to form organizations, these organizations then working together to lobby successfully for the needs of their children. The law is unique in several ways. There is no expiration date—it is regarded as permanent. It does more than just express a concern with handicapped children, it requires a specific commitment. The law sets forth as national policy the proposition that education must be extended to handicapped persons *as a fundamental right.*

Thanks to these parents, the right of the person with learning disabilities to a good education is now guaranteed by law. The challenge of today's parents is to insist on the transformation of this promise into reality.

Public Law 94-142: Education For All Handicapped Children Act

Because this law is so important to you, let me first explain what it includes, and then suggest how you can work within this law to be an advocate for your child or adolescent.

Handicapped children are defined as mentally retarded, hard-of-hearing, deaf, speech-impaired, visually handicapped, seriously emotionally disturbed, orthopedically impaired, or other health-impaired children, and *children with specific learning disabilities.*

The phrase "children with specific learning disabilities" is defined as applying to those children "who have a disorder in one or more of the basic psychological processes involved in understanding or in using language, spoken or written, which disorder may manifest itself in imperfect ability to listen, think, speak, read, write, spell, or do mathematical calculations. Such disorders include such conditions as perceptual handicaps, brain injury, minimal brain dysfunction, dyslexia, and developmental aphasia. Such term does not include children who have learning problems which are primarily the result of visual, hearing, or motor handicaps, of mental retardation, of emotional disturbance, or of environmental, cultural, or economic disadvantage."

Here is what these children and adolescents are entitled to:

1. A *free public education* is guaranteed to all between the ages of 3 and 21.

2. Each handicapped person is guaranteed an *"individualized education program,"* or IEP. This IEP must be in the form of a written statement, jointly developed by the school officials, the child's teacher, the parent or guardian, and if possible by the child her- or himself. It must include an analysis of the child's present achievement level, a list of both short-range and annual goals, an identification of the specific services that will be provided toward meeting these goals, and an indication of the extent to which the child will be able to participate in regular school programs. The IEP must also be clear about when

these services will be provided and how long they will last, and it provides a schedule for checking on the progress achieved under the plan and for making any revisions in it that may be needed.

3. Handicapped and nonhandicapped children must be educated together to the fullest extent that is appropriate. The child can be placed in special classes or separate schools only when the nature and severity of his or her handicap prevents satisfactory achievement in a regular education program.

4. Tests and other evaluation materials used in placing handicapped children must be prepared and administered in such a way as not to be racially or culturally discriminatory. They must also be presented in the child's native tongue.

5. An intensive and ongoing effort must be made to *locate* and *identify* children with handicaps, to *evaluate* their educational needs, and to *determine* whether these needs are being met.

6. In all efforts, *priority* must be given to those who are not receiving an education and to those severely handicapped people who are receiving an inadequate education.

7 In all decisions, a *prior consultation with the child's parents or guardians* must be held. No policies, programs, or procedures affecting the education of handicapped children may be adopted without a public notice.

8. These rights and guarantees apply to handicapped children in *private as well as public schools.* Note that any special education provided to any child shall be provided at no cost to the parents *if* state or local education agency officials placed the child in such schools or referred the child to them.

9. States and localities must develop comprehensive *personnel development programs,* including in-service training for regular as well as special-education teachers and support personnel.

10. In implementing the law, special effort shall be made to employ qualified handicapped persons.

11. All architectural barriers must be removed.

12. The state educaion agency has jurisdiction over all educational programs for handicapped children offered within
a given state, including those administered by non-
educational agencies, for example.

13. An *advisory panel* must exist to advise the state's education
agency of unmet needs. Membership *must include* handicapped people and parents or guardians of those people.

This law guarantees *procedural safeguards*. Parents or guardians
have an opportunity to examine any records that bear on the identification of a child as being handicapped, on the defined nature
and severity of their disability, and on the kind of educational
setting in which they are placed. Schools must provide written
notice prior to changing a child's placement. If a parent or guardian
objects to a school's decision, there must be a process in place
through which complaints can be registered. This process must
include an opportunity for an impartial hearing which offers parents rights similar to those involved in a court case—the right to
be advised by counsel (and by special-education experts if they
wish), to present evidence, to cross-examine witnesses, to compel
the presence of any witnesses who do not appear voluntarily, to
be provided a verbatim report of the proceedings, and to receive
the decision and findings in written form.

Your Child or Adolescent and Public Law 94-142

Each state has developed its own laws, rules, and regulations for
carrying out the intentions of this law. You will have to speak to
your school officials, other parents, or other knowledgeable people
to learn about the specifics as they apply in your state and community.

It is useful to look at the several steps in the process used to
help your son or daughter.

1. Search   Each school system should have a system for
seeking out students who might have a disability.

2. Find   Once a student with a potential problem is
identified, there should be a system for col-
lecting information and designing an evaluation process.

3. Evaluation   A comprehensive, multidisciplinary evaluation should be done.

4. Conference   Parents or guardians should meet with the school personnel and evaluation professionals to review the evaluation conclusions, any labels or diagnoses established, and any proposed placement and IEP. The details should be presented in writing.

5. Parent's decision process   Parents or guardians, with consultation from educational or other professionals and lawyers when needed, decide to accept, request clarification, request changes, or reject the proposed placement and IEP.

6. Appeals process   If parents reject the label, placement recommendation, or IEP, there should be an appeals process which starts with the local school system and can go to the county or state level.

7. Follow-up   *Progress reports* should be provided to the family. As the end of the school year approaches, a *reassessment* is done (with many school systems, a full, formal reevaluation is only done every three years). There should be a *conference* to plan the next year. Steps 5 and 6 are repeated before implementing the next year's plans.

Let's review each step in this process with your daughter or son in mind.

Search

If someone from your school system suggests that your son or daughter has a problem and wants to do some tests, be positive and agree to the testing. If the tests reveal a problem, you can get help. If the tests find nothing wrong, that should relieve both you and the school. If you are concerned about your child's academic progress and suspect a problem but the school has said nothing about it, speak to the classroom teacher. Share your observations and concerns.

If the teacher agrees with you, he or she must initiate the process of requesting a formal evaluation. If you cannot get the classroom teacher to start this process, meet with the principal. (It is better not to go directly to the principal first because this may antagonize the teacher.) When there are two parents, it is always better for both to be present at such meetings. Explain your concerns again, and ask the principal to start the evaluation process. If still nothing is done, call your school-system office or the Board of Education and ask to speak to the special education person responsible for your son or daughter's local school. Get this person's name, and insist on your right to speak to her or him. Explain your concerns and make it clear that you have already spoken to the teacher and the principal. Ask if the person you are talking to could observe your child and then meet with the teacher and you.

These efforts should result in an evaluation—or a very substantial reason why one is not required. If you are still not successful, several other strategies may work. You can get an evaluation privately. If significant results are found, they can be presented to the principal and the special-education staff. You could request time to meet with your school board and appeal to them, asking if they could help you get an evaluation for your child and determine whether or not your concerns are valid. Talk with other parents in your local chapter of the Association for Children with Learning Disabilities (see Appendix for listing). They can tell you what works in your school system.

The school may find it hard to identify certain types of children who are in difficulty. One is the quiet, shy, withdrawn student who doesn't cause any trouble. Unfortunately, the school may wait until this child is so frustrated and unhappy that he or she refuses to go to school, cries in class, or gets into trouble before they become concerned. With the parents' permission, of course, I have occasionally taught such children how to get into trouble—how to slam or throw books, yell at other kids or the teacher, refuse to do certain work, run out of class—just to get the kind of attention they need at school.

Another such type is the very bright child who manages to do at least average work in spite of his or her problems. This child may have a superior intelligence, but, because of learning disabilities, he or she performs at a C or D level. The school personnel see the child or adolescent as "just average," yet actually they are looking at a case of gross underachievement.

Some school systems throw yet another roadblock in your way. The law can be interpreted to read that a child must be at least three years behind to warrant an evaluation. What happens if your child is only in first, second, or third grade?

Don't accept this argument. Ask, "Must my child fail until the fourth grade to qualify for an evaluation?" And don't take "Yes" for an answer.

Find

Once the school agrees to the need for an evaluation, make yourself as informed as possible about what an evaluation is and what it should be. Find out what is planned, make sure that the plans are full-scale, and then prepare your son or daughter for each step. Be sure all the necessary members of the evaluation team have been called in. Review Chapters 9 and 10 on the evaluation to be certain you cover all the appropriate bases.

Conference

School personnel and special educators will meet with you. If you are two parents or guardians, be sure both of you are present when the school personnel, special educators, or the coordinator of the evaluating team meet with you. You may also bring legal counsel, your own professional consultants, or anyone else you feel you need. Angry, defensive, or demanding behavior won't get you anyplace. Assume that everyone there has the best interest of your son or daughter at heart. Listen, ask questions, reflect. Even if you agree completely with everything that is advised, ask for time to think and to read the recommendations in detail. On the one hand, anger or defensiveness polarizes the sides. On the other, too quick an agreement may prevent you from asking questions that occur to you after you read the reports and reflect on them.

Do your homework prior to the conference. Reread Chapters 9 and 10. Talk with other parents who have been in the same situation and, if possible, learn something about what programs are likely to be suggested.

During the conference, ask questions. If someone says that your child has learning disabilities, ask for specifics. You know what learning disabilities are. Impress them with your awareness and their need to be precise. Don't let the evaluator(s) overwhelm you with words. Ask for definitions and clarification in a calm, concerned way. Let them know that although what they say is important, this is *your* child or adolescent about whom you care very much.

If you don't agree with the findings, don't challenge them just now. Tell the evaluator that you would like a copy of the test results to show to another professional for a second opinion. You wouldn't consent to your child having heart surgery or even to being sent to the hospital without a second opinion. Committing your child to at least one year of a special-education program has just as great an impact on his or her life.

You will have to agree to the diagnosis, or label—that is, to the name your school gives to the problems they say your son or daughter has. You will also have to agree to the placement recommended and the Individualized Education Program (IEP) proposed. If a name for your child's condition is used, ask for the school's definition of this label, in writing, along with the criteria they use to apply it. Read this statement over carefully to see if the description actually fits your child.

Keep in mind the difference between an emotional problem that *causes* academic difficulties and an emotional problem that *results from* an academic difficulty. If your son's or daughter's behavior problems are due to the frustrations and failures experienced because of learning disabilities, don't let the school label the child only "emotionally disturbed." This might well be a secondary diagnosis, along with the learning disabilities, but it should not be the *only* diagnosis. Don't accept it if you believe that it is wrong. Mislabeling not only misses the correct issue, it can easily result in an inappropriate placement and the wrong IEP.

The school is responsible for placing your child in an appropriate program within their system. Only if this is not possible will they consider an out-of-system, or private, placement. You may prefer that your child go into a particular private program that you know about. The school does not have to concur, however, if an appropriate placement is available within their own system. You might argue that the private placement is better, and this might be true. But even if it were, the law states only that each child must receive an *appropriate* education, not necessarily the *best* education possible.

As I said in Chapter 11, there are several program levels. You want to find the *least restrictive program* that still provides the *most effective educational support* for your child. Remember that this does not always mean being in a program that resembles a regular class program. The least restrictive environment for some children might be the most restrictive environment available. For example, a child may need the security and support of a small, separate, self-contained classroom in order to feel safe enough to relax and become available for learning. For this child, the most restrictive environment is the least restrictive environment in which to learn and progress.

Ask for the details of any placement. Where is it? Will your child have to be transported out of the neighborhood? Ask about the qualifications of the teacher, the size and age distribution of the class, and the mix of kids scheduled for the class—diagnosis, level of intellectual function, and so on. Ask if you can visit the program. Even if it is spring and you will see a different group of students, you will get a feel for what goes on. Try to speak to several parents of the children currently in the program. If the teacher has not yet been selected, ask for a written statement of the qualifications that teacher must have. In the fall, check to see that the one selected meets the requirements.

What about the IEP? This is the written plan identifying the instruction designed especially for your son or daughter and listing reasonable expectations for the child's achievement. This document should also include a system for monitoring progress:

At a minimum, each IEP must cover the following points:

1. A statement of your child or adolescent's levels of educational performance.
2. A statement of yearly goals or achievements expected by the end of the school year.
3. Short-term objectives stated in instructional terms which are the steps leading to the mastery of these yearly goals.
4. A statement of the specific special education and support services to be provided to the child.
5. A statement of the extent to which a child will be able to participate in regular educational programs and justification for any special placement recommended.
6. Projected dates for initiation of services and the anticipated duration of the services.
7. A statement of the criteria and evaluation procedures to be used in determining, on at least an annual basis, whether short-term objectives are being achieved.

In addition to an appropriate placement and IEP, your child or adolescent may need other services. These are called *related services,* and they are to be provided at no expense to the parents. The formal definition of related services is "transportation and such developmental, corrective, and other supportive services (including speech pathology and audiology, psychological services, physical and occupational therapy, recreation, and medical counseling services, except that such medical services shall be for diagnostic and evaluation purposes only) as may be required to assist a handicapped child to benefit from special education, and includes the early identification and assessment of handicapping conditions in children." These services are usually provided by the school system and built into the school program.

For example, individual, group, or family therapy might be recommended. Sometimes placement in a residential treatment center (a boarding-school-like program designed to help emotionally disturbed people) is suggested. If any related services are proposed, work with your school. They may offer to provide help within their own system, or they may refer you to a facility that works with them. If you have medical insurance, your school personnel may ask that this plan cover some of the cost. Whatever the arrangement, however, you should not bear the cost.

And related services are costly. Some school systems carefully avoid recommending help of this kind. If the school personnel do make such recommendations in the IEP, the school must pay. If the school avoids direct statements to this effect, it may mean that you will have to seek such help at your own expense.

The Parents' Decision Process

After the conference, you are entitled to a full transcript of the meeting. You can also get copies of all tests that were done. The placement and the IEP recommendations must also be provided in writing.

Read all of the documents. If necessary, ask for clarification or more details. Seek consultation and advice from other parents or from professionals. Visit the program proposed. When appropriate, share all of the information you have gathered with the child in question.

If you are comfortable with the school's plan for your child or adolescent, you may agree to it and sign the necessary documents. If you do not agree and cannot get the school personnel to modify their proposals, inform them that you wish to appeal. You are entitled by law to due process of appeal.

The Appeals Process

The appeals process differs with each state and local school system. Ask the school personnel to provide a written statement of just what your rights are and what the process involves. Discuss your options and strategies with your local Association for Children with Learning Disabilities if possible. You may choose to seek legal counsel. Find out from other parents of children with learning disabilities which attorneys in your area are most knowledgeable about education and special-education law.

Each step of an appeal will be like a re-creation of the original conference. The school will present its material and the reasons for its decisions. You will present your side of the story, where you differ with the school, and what you want. The appeals board will agree either with the school or with you, or it may suggest an alternative, or compromise, for both sides to consider.

As you move up the ladder from the local school system to the county and then to the state, the members of the appeals groups will be less and less involved with local issues—school board politics, school budgets—and they may take a more impartial look at the issues and the child involved.

The appeals process may go quickly or it may take months. An appeal all the way up to the state level may take a year or more. Meanwhile your son or daughter's education must go on. You might decide to accept a placement and IEP under protest, allowing an educational program to begin while the appeals process proceeds. Or you might place your child in a private program using your own money while waiting for the appeals process to be completed.

Implementation

The best designed plans laid in April and May may fall apart in September. Be observant when school opens. Be sure the placement, the teacher, the related services, and the IEP are correct and in operation. Be concerned, ask questions, but try not to be a nuisance. If you believe that some departure from the plan agreed upon has been made, contact the special-education staff and ask for clarification.

Be sure that the regular classroom teachers with whom your child has contact are aware of any special needs or programs. Be certain that they are familiar with the evaluation and the IEP and that they are in regular contact with the special-education teachers.

The IEP lists short-term goals and sets up criteria for measuring progress toward them. If the teacher or the teaching team do not get in touch with you, ask for conferences monthly or at least every other month. And ask for progress reports on the same schedule.

Programs begun in September tend to get changed or diluted. Ask your son or daughter to keep you informed, or check this for yourself. Does the speech therapist see your child twice a week for forty-five minutes or has it slipped to once a week? Does the learning disability specialist still see the child privately thirty minutes every day? Or is it now three times a week, or along with other children? Know your child's IEP and insist that the child get what it promises. No changes can be made without a written notification and your concurrence.

As each school year comes to a close, be sure that a conference is scheduled to plan the next year. Each new plan requires the same formal process, along with your formal concurrence.

Other Thoughts

Your son or daughter must be kept informed. How much you share, what you explain, and how you explain it will depend on the child's age. If you need help, ask the professionals involved to meet with you and your child or adolescent. If you think it would be helpful, make it a family session.

I touched earlier on how to handle any resistance by your son or daughter to accepting help. Let me mention one other problem—*stigma*. Other children can be cruel, sometimes on purpose, sometimes they just say all the wrong things. The special programs may be called "retard" or "mental" classes, and the children in them may be called "speds," for *special education*. It all hurts. Speak to the teachers. If necessary, speak to the parents of an offending child as positively as you can. (Here, as elsewhere, hostility won't get you very far.) Support your child and empathize with his or her feelings. Don't be afraid to show your own emotions, and don't be afraid to have a good cry together. You would do anything in the world to spare the child these problems—but, they exist. Make sure the child knows that you care too much to ignore them and that you will do everything possible to support and help.

At the risk of being perseverative, I must again emphasize the importance of being an *informed consumer* and an *assertive advocate*.

Nowhere is this more critical than with the issues we have just examined.

No matter how dedicated the school's staff, they can never care as much about your son or daughter as you do. Work closely with them. And make them do their work. If you become their colleagues, working together toward a common goal, they will do an even better job of helping your child or adolescent reach his or her maximum growth and potential.

Part Six

Summary

16

In Conclusion

Perhaps you remember Victor, the boy whose victorious story opened this book.

Let us for a moment look at another young man who had the same extent of learning disabilities. Bob struggled through elementary school, did poorly in junior high school, and finally quit school at sixteen. Early on, his parents tried to get the school to provide help. Later, they gave up in frustration. Once he quit school, they lost control and lost track of him.

The next time they heard of him, he had been arrested for killing two policemen while trying to rob a bank.

The newspaper coverage was painfully revealing (*Washington Post*, August 8, 1976). The psychiatric report noted, "Every time he struggled hopelessly with a math problem, every time he stumbled over a sentence from his first reader, every time his brother beat him in a fight . . . [he] grew a little more hostile, a little more withdrawn, a little more convinced of his worthlessness. . . . He thought of himself as stupid and worthless and developed intense anger at himself and the world."

Bob's parents were professionals. His older brother was an honors student. Bob had been labeled "slow" in elementary school, but the first testing was not done until eighth grade. It revealed learning disabilities and an IQ in the bright range. No programs were offered. The high-school counselor never knew of these studies. After Bob quit school, he moved from job to job. He spent more and more time riding his motorcycle and getting into trouble with the police. The bank robbery and killings were an almost inevitable outcome of his life-style.

Bob is now in prison.

You have probably heard all this before, but let me mention a few other people with learning disabilities before getting to my point. Leonardo da Vinci often wrote backward: His writing shows evidence of perceptual problems. Woodrow Wilson didn't learn the alphabet until he was eight; he didn't read until he was eleven. At school, he excelled only in work that was related to speech. He was labeled as "dull and backward."

Auguste Rodin, the famous artist-sculptor, did poorly with math and spelling. He was described as "ineducable" and "an idiot." General George Patton was severely learning disabled and could not read or write at age twelve. A special reader worked with him all through his time at West Point. Winston Churchill had learning disabilities. Albert Einstein did not talk until age four or read until age nine. He was considered backward and made progress only after his family moved him to a special school where he could learn using his own style.

Thomas Edison couldn't learn anything in public school. He entered at age eight and was removed three months later by his mother who decided to teach him herself. His autobiography is revealing. "I remember I used never to be able to get along at school. I was always at the foot of the class. I used to feel that the teachers did not sympathize with me and that my father thought I was stupid." Later, he added, "It was impossible to observe and learn the processes of nature by description, or the English alphabet and arithmetic only by rote . . . it was always necessary to observe with my own eyes and to do things or to make things. . . ." To see for himself, to test things for himself, he said, was, "for one instance . . . better than to learn about something I had never seen for 2 hours." His mother noted that he never learned to spell. His grammar and syntax were appalling. He was hard to teach. Whatever he learned, he learned in his own way. In fact, she said, she only inspired him—no one ever taught him anything. He taught himself.

There are others. Perhaps you have met successful people who overcame or learned to compensate for their learning disabilities. Perhaps you are one. I know that I am. You should have seen the first draft of this book—spelling errors, letter reversals, illegible handwriting. But I have something now that I didn't have when I was in school. I have a secretary who has learned to read my handwriting, who can spell, and who no longer laughs at my errors. That is compensation. But I did not always have such help. My grades in elementary and junior high school were less than good. The only reason I did not get tracked into a vocational high school was that my mother met with the principal and demanded that I have a chance in the regular high school. She won. Or, I should say, she gave me the chance to win. Somehow I got my act together in high school. I taught myself how to learn and how to pass exams. That, for me, was the beginning. The ending never comes. I still face new frustrations and challenges. Recently I was at a Congressional hearing related to budget. I needed to pass information to someone who was answering a Senator's questions. When I got my note back, on the top it said "Thanks"—then he proceeded to correct two spelling errors and one reversal.

What determines the outcome for us? Why is it that some children and adolescents make it and some do not? It seems to me that the outcome depends on the interaction of several factors:

1. The types and the extent of learning disabilities.
2. The level of intellectual potential.
3. The time when these disabilities are recognized and an appropriate program developed. If this is not done early, additional academic and emotional problems develop. The child grows farther and farther behind.
4. The kinds of help provided in school and in the family.
5. The child or adolescent's personality. Does he or she take on the disabilities as a challenge, accept the need to work harder, develop styles of coping? Does he or she relate in a way that makes people want to reach out and help or in a way that pushes them away? And, finally,
6. The parents' and the whole family's ability to be supportive and caring.

Current research efforts will someday give us the knowledge to minimize or prevent learning disabilities and to improve the existing problems through education, medication, and/or special nutritional approaches. For now there is little that we can do to "cure" the learning disabilities your daughter or son has. Her or his intellectual potential is established. You can only work for programs that will maximize this potential.

Our best hope for achieving the best outcome is to work on the other factors that affect the child—those factors that we *can* influence.

By being an *informed consumer* and an *assertive advocate* you can work to get the necessary evaluations and school interventions. Through your own understanding, you can help your child or adolescent understand and maximize strengths rather than magnify weaknesses. You can help with his or her self-image and personality development. You can help your family understand and support the child. You can support your other children. And, equally important, you can support yourself.

I hope that this book has given you more understanding than you had when you began it. I hope that it has suggested a new way of thinking and some ideas that will help you help your son or daughter reach his or her full potential as a happy, healthy, productive adult. That will never be easy, but I wish you the best of success.

Appendix

Resources

Parent Organizations

Association for Children and Adults with Learning Disabilities
This organization, referred to as "ACLD," is a national parent association with state and local chapters. Membership is open to parents and professionals. The local groups provide educational programs, advice on local issues and programs, and support systems for parents, families, and the children and adolescents. To find your nearest chapter, contact the National Office:

4156 Library Road
Pittsburgh, Pennsylvania 15234
(412) 340-1515

The Orton Dyslexia Society
This organization is for parents of children and adults with dyslexia, as well as professionals concerned with dyslexia.

724 York Road
Baltimore, Maryland 21204
(301) 296-0232

Other Useful Organizations

American Association of Children's Residential Centers
This organization represents most of the residential treatment centers available for children and adolescents.

P.O. Box 14188
Ben Franklin Station
13th and Pennsylvania Avenue, N.W.
Washington, D.C. 20044

American Association of Psychiatric Services for Children
This organization represents many of the programs and organizations providing mental health services for children.

1725 K Street, N.W.
Washington, D.C. 20036

Council for Exceptional Children
This is the branch of the National Education Association for educators in special education.

1920 Association Drive
Reston, Virginia 22091

Epilepsy Foundation of America
An organization for parents of children and adults with seizure disorders.

4351 Garden City Drive
Landover, Maryland 20785

Foundation for Children with Learning Disabilities
An organization that does extensive fund raising. This money is used to support research on and demonstration programs for children with learning disabilities.

99 Park Avenue
New York, New York 10016

National Association for Retarded Citizens
An organization for parents of retarded children and adults.

2709 Avenue E East
Arlington, Texas 76011

National Congress of Parents and Teachers
This is the national organization representing parent-teacher groups
throughout the country.

700 North Rush Street
Chicago, Illinois 60611

National Council of Community Mental Health Centers
This organization represents most of the Community Mental Health
Centers in the country.

2233 Wisconsin Avenue, N.W.
Suite 322
Washington, D.C. 20007

National Mental Health Association
This organization consists of volunteers concerned with the mental-
health needs of the country. It has state and local chapters.

1800 North Kent Street
Arlington, Virginia 22209

National Society for Autistic Children
An organization for parents of autistic children and adults.

1234 Massachusetts Avenue, N.W.
Washington, D.C. 20005

Parents Without Partners
A national organization with local chapters for parents raising children alone.

7910 Woodmont Avenue, N.W.
Washington, D.C. 20014

United Cerebral Palsy Association
An organization for parents with cerebral palsy children and adults.

66 East 34th Street
New York, New York 10016

Professional Organizations

Each of the following organizations represents a specific professional group. You might want to contact one to ask about the qualifications of a particular individual, to ask for recommendations of professionals you might use, or, for general information.

American Academy of Child Psychiatry

3615 Wisconsin Avenue, N.W.
Washington, D.C. 20016

American Academy of Neurology

4015 W. 65th Street
Suite 302
Minneapolis, Minnesota 55435

American Academy of Ophthalmology

1100 17th Street, N.W.
Washington, D.C. 20036

American Academy of Pediatrics

1801 Hinman Avenue
Evanston, Illinois 60204

American Medical Association

535 N. Dearborn
Chicago, Illinois 60610

American Nurses' Association

134 W. 78th Street
New York, New York 10024

American Occupational Therapy Association

> 1383 Piccard Drive
> Rockville, Maryland 20850

American Optometric Association

> 243 North Lindberg
> St. Louis, Missouri 63141

American Psychiatric Association

> 1700 18th Street, N.W.
> Washington, D.C. 20036

American Psychological Association

> Division 22, Psychological Aspects of Disabilities
> 1200 17th Street, N.W.
> Washington, D.C. 20036

American Speech, Language, and Hearing Association

> 10801 Rockville Pike
> Rockville, Maryland 20852

American Society for Adolescent Psychiatry

> 24 Green Valley Road
> Wallingford, Pennsylvania 19086

National Association of School Psychologists

> 2953 Silver Lake Boulevard
> Cuyahoga Falls, Ohio 44224

National Association of Social Workers

> 7981 Eastern Avenue
> Silver Spring, Maryland 20910

Legal Organizations

Many law schools have special units or programs offering reference materials or counsel on handicapped children. If you or your attorney needs such help, contact your nearest law school and find out what they offer. The following list of national programs may be of help or provide a local resource.

American Coalition of Citizens with Disabilities

> 1200 15th Street, N.W.
> Washington, D.C. 20036

Children's Defense Fund

> 1520 New Hampshire Avenue, N.W.
> Washington, D.C. 20036

Mental Disability Legal Resource Center

> American Bar Association
> 1800 M Street, N.W.
> Washington, D.C. 20036

Colleges and Other Post-High-School Training

The number of programs and the kinds of programs available change and increase all the time. Rather than list those programs in existence when this book was being prepared, here are some resources you can contact to get a current list.

You can also contact the Graduate School of Education at your nearest university. Ask for the Department of Special Education. The faculty of this department can advise you of resources or people at their school or others.

A National Directory of Four Year Colleges, Two Year Colleges, and Post High School Training Programs for Young People with Learning Disabilities, edited by P. M. Fielding.
This publication lists each type of program itemized in its title. It can be obtained from:

> Partners in Publishing
> Box 50347
> Tulsa, Oklahoma 74150
> (918) 584-5906

Association for Children and Adults with Learning Disabilities
This organization provides a current list of colleges with special programs for students with learning disabilities.

4156 Library Road
Pittsburgh, Pennsylvania 15234
(412) 340-1515

Special Note

To obtain the specific details on how your son or daughter can take the Scholastic Aptitude Test (SAT) untimed, with a preceptor, and/or with other special considerations, contact the organization that develops and conducts the test:

College Board
American Testing Program
Box 592
Princeton, New Jersey 08541

Index

About the Author

Larry B. Silver, M.D., a child psychiatrist, is Acting Director of the National Institute of Mental Health (NIMH) as well as a Clinical Professor of Psychiatry at Georgetown University School of Medicine. Prior to coming to NIMH in 1979 he was Professor of Psychiatry, Professor of Pediatrics, and Chief of Child Psychiatry at Rutgers Medical School.

His area of special concern and interest over the past twenty years has been children and adolescents with learning disabilities, and their families. He is on the Professional Advisory Board of the Association for Children with Learning Disabilities and on the Professional Advisory Board of the Foundation for Children with Learning Disabilities.

The views Dr. Silver expresses in this book do not necessarily reflect the positions of the National Institute of Mental Health.